"*Omni Reveals the Four Principles of Creation* is a thoughtful, worthwhile book with much to offer."
—Joya Pope, author of *The World According to Michael, An Old Soul's Guide to the Universe* and *Upcoming Changes*

"This book contains many gems and much food for thought."
—Shepherd Hoodwin, author of *The Journey of Your Soul*.

"In the tradition of guides such as Seth and Orin, Omni, a wise guide brought through John Payne, encourages and inspires us with his words of loving wisdom to fulfill our potential and to create a life of joy, love, and abundance. He shows us how to read the meaning and message behind the events of our lives (and in the greater universe) so we can create the reality we want and learn from what we have created."
—Sanaya Roman, author of *Living with Joy*

Lindis - Chloc Guinness 2002

OMNI REVEALS
THE FOUR
PRINCIPLES
OF CREATION

John L. Payne

FINDHORN
Press

First published by Findhorn Press in 2001

ISBN 1 899171 88 6

British Library Cataloguing-in-Publication Data.
A catalogue record for this book is available from the British Library.

Library of Congress Catalog Card Number: 00-109406

Edited by Tony Mitton
Layout by Pam Bochel
Front cover design by Dale Vermeer

Printed and bound in Finland

Published by
Findhorn Press

The Park, Findhorn
Forres IV36 3TY
Scotland
Tel 01309 690582
Fax 01309 690036

P.O. Box 13939
Tallahassee
Florida 32317-3939, USA
Tel 850 893 2920
Fax 850 893 3442

e-mail info@findhornpress.com
findhornpress.com

Contents

Foreword

From the moment that the concept of channelling was known to me I knew that it was what I wanted to do with my life. The idea that it was possible to consciously tap into higher wisdom and to get answers from an inexhaustible source of knowledge excited me and seemed to be the answer to all the questions that religion had left me asking. I devoured the Seth books by Jane Roberts, and Seth became a dear friend, as I read his words almost daily. I so much wanted to have my own Seth!

As a child, I was very sensitive and had several "imaginary" friends. I have always had a sense of the spiritual and would tell my parents that I wanted to be a priest when I grew up. Today, I fulfil this role as a teacher and now as the writer of this book, for it has always been my passion to communicate "the things of God" to as many people as possible. Growing up with religion, I was often vexed by the teachings that stated that God was a superior and jealous being, out to punish us if we did not obey. These teachings simply did not fit in with my experience of "God", for I knew that somewhere there was a source of boundless and endless love, and all I had to do was to find out where it was!

I have now discovered that all true wisdom comes from within and that the most important thing for all of us is not our desire to be loved, but our desire to love. When Omni and his group of non-physical teachers first came into my life, they challenged many of my beliefs and assumptions. As a gatherer of information, a life-long habit, I began to see that some of the information I had gathered was not correct, and that other information was but one tiny piece of a very large puzzle.

I encourage you not to focus on the source from which this book claims to come, but on the wisdom within. Neither Omni nor I seek to become gurus, or indeed claim to have the sole rights to Universal Truths. To quote Omni, they say "There are but two truths: 'You are deeply and exquisitely loved' and 'You create your own reality'; all the rest is perception based upon the experience of the being in question, whether physical or non-physical." I, as the channeller of this book, encourage you to take that which speaks directly to your heart and either discard or re-visit the rest at another time.

This book has been birthed as a result of 6 years of travelling and channelling. My adventure started back in 1992 when I visited a hypnotherapist to help me stop smoking (which I did). After my first hypnosis, my psychic abilities suddenly awakened, culminating in out of body experiences, and I became aware of things that I had previously not noticed. Then one day, in January 1993, a wonderful book came into my life 'by chance'. This book was *Opening to Channel* by Sanaya Roman and Duane Packer. It literally changed my life. I went on to study Light Body with Sanaya and Duane and later became a Light Body teacher and trance channel myself. My work has taken me to four continents and to countries that have touched my soul deeply, notably South Africa. Each country I have visited has taught me unique lessons and has expanded my abilities as a teacher. The questions in this book, and Omni's answers, are based on the questions most frequently asked over these past six years, and it is with great joy and the deepest gratitude to Omni that I offer you these answers for your consideration.

My deepest wish is that you will be touched in some way by this book: that your heart may be opened in an area that may have been closed, or that you experience acceptance at a deeper level, or gain a sense of joy and excitement. I for one celebrate the fact that all is well in our world and that above all things, love prevails.

With many thanks,

John L. Payne
Channel for Omni

Chapter 1

Who or What is Omni?

To answer this question in terms that you can grasp more easily, we need to explain different levels of consciousness, for the Universe is multidimensional, as indeed are you. There are many levels of consciousness beyond the physical state, just as there are many levels of consciousness within the physical. You do acknowledge, do you not, that a goat and a horse have different levels of awareness and consciousness? Similarly, all that is non-physical have such different levels. However, in the physical mode, the majority of you view differing levels of consciousness as superior or inferior, or better or worse. It does not happen this way in the non-physical world, for our experience in the non-physical is of the union with all life. In this union, we do not experience 'inferior' or 'superior' levels. We simply acknowledge a different and unique expression of All-That-Is. Human beings are preoccupied with hierarchy and what might be termed pecking order. We are not. It is not that you are 'wrong' to do this, for hierarchy makes logical sense when viewing your world from the physical perspective, for your physical senses tell you that a tree is 'less intelligent' than you are. In that way, you are correct. Viewed from the broader view of all life that we have gained, and continue to gain, such a statement is untrue. More is not necessarily better.

The non-physical world has been described by many, and our description may differ somewhat, but it is largely terminology that makes the difference. The Universe is a vast and complex place, with many levels, many worlds, and many realities. Therefore, there are multiple ways in which to describe the non-physical. Let us give you these definitions. First, there is the Physical, then the Emotional (Astral), then the Mental (Causal), then the Spiritual planes of existence. There are many levels existing within these three main non-physical areas. There are seven levels in total, and each of those seven levels is broken down into seven sub-levels. For simplicity, we speak of three non-physical dimensions: Astral, Mental, and Spiritual. The Spiritual is further divided into the Higher Mental and what we would call the Christ and Buddhaic. Beyond and within those are what we call the 'multidimensional realities'. Each of you is aware of these levels at one level or another of your own consciousness. These areas are not secrets, for each of you has been present in each of these levels and many of you are touching or glimpsing into these realities during your meditations. We are Omni, and we form a bridge of consciousness between that which has been called Christ Consciousness and that which has been called Buddhaic Consciousness.

Christ Consciousness is about expressing the acceptance of unity with all life, and allowing emotional unity. Buddhaic Consciousness is about experiencing that same oneness by 'embracing' it in the mind, knowing that all exists in the mind of God. It is a challenge to express this in words; we transmit energies to assist others to experience these levels through meditation. In the experience of the Christ, you may say, "I accept all as my brother and sister. As I love one, I love myself; as I hurt one, I hurt myself. I see that we are all of the same stuff, we are one." In the experience of Buddha, you say, "I understand that All-That-Is is alive within me." This is the essential difference. One is not higher than the other. They are merely a shift of focus, just as you are focused in physical reality, not really there, simply focused.

We form this bridge and communicate the ideas and concepts contained within. Humanity is at a stage where many of you are able to experience these states of being, albeit for limited periods, often for several minutes. As you are now able to reach these levels energetically by shifting your vibration to align with those of us focused here, we are now in a position to communicate the ideas of our focus to you. As humanity continues to grow, or to shift its focus towards unity rather than isolation, we are responding to that shift by giving you that which you now seek. This comes in the form of teaching.

The Universe is a place of vibration. As you shift your focus, you shift your vibration, and as you shift your focus away from what you have been doing towards something new, you begin to align with that new thing. In this way, you have 'invited' non-physical beings such as myself to enter your focus, albeit only a small portion, so that we may share our knowledge with you.

In this realm, we do not act as individuals, but act as a part of a group or consensus reality. We are bonded to one another mentally and emotionally. We know each other's every thought, idea, aspiration, and experience. This may sound odd, even frightening to you, or even appear as an invasion of privacy. But we have no concept of privacy, for privacy exists only where shame resides. We have nothing to hide and seek not to hide anything. We do have a kind of etiquette in which we seek 'permission' to share totally in another's experience. This is rarely, if ever, denied, but one of our number may choose to create an experience that is more solitary. Although we are a group consciousness, made up of 343 individual multidimensional beings, we have the ability to appear to you as if we are one. If your eyes could pierce the veil that separates you from the non-physical world, you would perceive, for the most part, a handsome being approximately ten feet tall clothed in long white robes with a very bright light emanating from his chest and forehead areas. We speak to you as one, with one unified voice, with one unified consciousness. We have a spokesperson for our group, we call him Omni-Emmanuel, and this one is the communicator, the holder of focus for our group, but considers us to be Omni.

Why do you use the name Omni?

We use the name Omni because we are all things to all people. We experience unity with all life and truly understand that all exists within the mind of God. As we are one with the mind of God, we are understanding, and indeed experiencing, that you exist within our minds. We are not only communicating with you, but we are the dust under your feet, the wind in your hair, the smile of a child, the majesty of an aged oak. We are Omni.

Have you ever had a life on Earth? Are you a dead person?

Dead? Far from dead! There is no dead; there is only shifting of focus. To answer your question, we have to say yes and no. We, as Omni, have never been present in a physical body. If we had, then you would have recognized us as a seer, a prophet, or a messiah, for when one from our level of focus chooses physical existence, there is always great fanfare and the impact of such 'visitations' are felt for years to come. Jesus and the Buddha are cases in point. No, we have not been physically present. However, just as we are united in oneness with all at this level, then the answer is, "Yes," for Jesus, Buddha, Krishna, and some others have all walked in the shoes of men. The individual 'parts' that make up our group have been physically present, but for the most part, not on what you call Earth. There are many, many civilisations across your galaxy and countless other galaxies in which consciousness chooses to focus. We have been focused on one other world and have completed the mastering of that world many, many aeons ago. This does not make us an 'extraterrestrial' in the way that you would have it, for we are not presently in that form, but we have had association with other planets.

What is your interest in Earth and why are you speaking with us now?

The Universe is a place of vibration, of energy. It is our intention to impart knowledge to all those who seek, so that they may be assisted in shifting their focus towards that which is increasingly joyful and pleasing to them. You, focused in your reality, have in past decades shifted your attention and focus away from what you know in search of new answers. Our intent to impart information and your intent to receive new information has created a vibrational match. You could say that you have invited us here, although we do understand that the invitation was not personal. We have a common purpose and our common purpose has brought us together.

Your planet is in the midst of an evolutionary shift towards unity consciousness. That unity consciousness is akin to the unity consciousness that we speak of when describing our focus or reality. You will not experience the same oneness as we do, for your physical apparatus limits you. All stages of consciousness in physical reality are mirrored in the non-physical and vice versa. As you shift your focus towards the experiencing of unity consciousness, you automatically draw our attention to yourselves. Let us put it this way: if a high school student and a university student were both to study math, they would indeed be focused on the same subject, simply at different levels—from our perspective, not higher or lower—but the analogy assists us to explain in terms readily understandable to you.

There have been many predictions made about this time frame, mostly inaccurate in terms of the way in which change will occur. We do not foresee great catastrophes and Earth changes that will destroy civilisation as you know it. What we do see is a rapidly changing political and social landscape as your focus shifts even more towards unity consciousness. Some will experience natural disasters, for these have also been the tools through which you have chosen to learn. Is it not the case that you are apt to live next to someone for several years before you even know that person's name? In our observation, when disaster strikes, you are apt to reach out and touch one another. As this is the manner of your seeking, you may continue to create war, widespread disease, and natural disasters until you choose as a species to achieve what you want without adding the ingredient of pain. Pain and struggle are not necessary, but they will remain until you decide that they no longer give you what you want and that you can achieve more without them.

Do we need to be afraid of this process?

Certainly not! It is consciousness, thought, that creates circumstance, that creates worlds and destroys them. Choose to shift your focus freely and with ease, and free and easy it will be. It is as simple as that. Your mind, the 'you' that exists in your head so to speak, moulds universal energy with thought in order to create a world in which you can live. Your world, like our world, exists within the mind of God, within your mind. It is as real as you want it to be. Envision joyful expansion into new consciousness, and it will be yours. Assume that the transition into the New World will be challenging and full of disasters, and this too will be yours. It makes no difference what the majority is thinking; your unique world, which is you, cannot be touched by 'them' unless you invite them in the same way as you have invited us, that is, by directing your attention to the subject. The Universe always delivers unto you that which you focus on.

Imagine that the Universe is like a huge puppy dog that is in and around everything, and its only desire is to please and respond to its owner, you. With your every thought, you send a command to this puppy dog who is delighted to comply. If you focus on disaster, the Universe will deliver that to you as gladly as it will deliver peace and prosperity to you. It cannot be any other way, for that is the nature of the Universe in which you live.

What will this New World look like?

It will look exactly as you choose it to look. But from our perspective, knowing that you are shifting your focus towards unity consciousness, we can tell you that all forms in your world will begin to reflect that shift in focus. These forms are government, education systems, science, medicine, industry, agriculture, and finance. All will be transformed by your shift in focus.

This shift is taking place because there are 'new' parts of your being that are awakening within you. When as a species you sent out a request for more understanding of who you are, your greater self, your soul, responded and began to penetrate your world more deeply, emerging further into your day-to-day consciousness. Just as we are multidimensional in nature, so are you. You are non-physical in nature and the physical you is an extension of that non-physical being. As you sent out your request, your non-physical part responded by projecting more of itself into you, therefore bringing you the consciousness that you seek. You are the creator of your own reality; you even create the expanded consciousness that you seek. It is not something that you find; it is something that you create and draw to you through your desire for it. Not only do you learn and grow, but also you create the learning process and choose how to learn and create the growth. You, like us, are creators. Nothing more, and nothing less.

Your New World will see greater harmony between the animal kingdom and humanity, and many teachers will spring forth amongst you to assist you in bridging the gap you have created for yourselves. The relationship to dolphins and other cetaceans will transform the relationships between humans and all other life forms on the planet. The mass realisation that dolphins think and feel as you do will change your view of the world. This will be the first step in understanding that you are not alone. For when dolphin language is interpreted, understood, and communicated to humanity as a whole, much contemplation will follow. They will speak to you of the things that you speak of. Expect dolphins to be like humans in many ways. There are those who are intellectual, those who are spiritual, and those who are frivolous, just like there are amongst you. This revelation will send out shock waves for some, and elation and joy for others.

These creatures will communicate to you their history, your history, and what their relationship is to the planet and all life. They will be your teachers, just as you will also be teachers to many of them. For the first time you will have a relationship with a sentient being that is not human, that is not of your species. This will change you forever, and it will change how you look at your position in the Universe. You will no longer be alone. Once you have bridged this gap, and have embraced non-humanoid terrestrial beings as 'brothers' and 'sisters', you will be ready to embrace other forms that exist beyond that which you call Earth, but not before.

The realisation of your connection to all life will urge you to assess your treatment of other species. Agriculture in particular will be transformed, as your relationship to plants and animals becomes one of stewardship and cooperation rather than subjugation. It is this move that explains the great interest in dolphins in recent years in your world, for the dolphins and other cetaceans hold one of the most important keys to your evolution.

"You have evolved more in the past 100 years than you have in the past 2,000 years!"

You will begin to experience that what you do in one part of the world affects all other parts of the world, and the wealthy countries of the world will begin to understand that their wealth is not solid or enduring whilst there is still poverty. It is not that you will be urged to give away all your worldly goods, but your trading practices based upon beliefs in lack will transform to create equilibrium. With these changes, the political landscape will change. In some areas of the world, this change will be smooth and relatively uneventful. In other areas, there will be resistance, fear, and what we might term a bumpy ride. We anticipate that the transformation of the planet will take another 50–100 years. You are already moving at breakneck speed, and you have evolved more in the past 100 years than you have in the past 2,000 years!

You are talking about 'evolution' and change, but what is the purpose of all this, and why are we evolving in the first place?

First, let us make it clear, you are not evolving in order to become worthy of some spiritual hierarchy; you are not here to prove yourselves worthy of God. You are here by choice; you have not been placed here nor have you been obliged to come here. What is your purpose for being in the physical state? It is simply to master this reality, which is one of many. Indeed you have already mastered many different realities and belief systems. This is but another focus you have chosen. When we speak of mastering, we speak of creating an experience which is joyful and which takes you to ever-increasing vibrations. This is the driving force of all life. You enter this world, for the most part, at a low vibration. At this vibration, you are unable to perceive much beyond yourself and your immediate surroundings. We could equate this level of experience to that of 'primitive' peoples whose entire focus is upon the physical, and survival within the physical. As time passes and you gain more experience within this focus, you broaden your view and begin to 'see' other aspects of this focus. You begin to see other objects and how these objects relate not only to you, but also to others. With this increasing viewpoint, you raise your vibration accordingly so that this broader perspective can be consciously interpreted.

This is a game you are playing; it is nothing more than that. You are here to see if you can hold the very broadest focus and still remain in the physical mode. The very broadest focus at this level of the game is to understand that you are one with All-That-Is and physically focused. This state of being, of winning the game, is what many have called spiritual enlightenment. There have been many who have won the game, notably Jesus and the Buddha, amongst others. Because it is a game, you *can* choose to stop playing the game whenever you wish to. There are those who, after leaving the focus of their physical bodies in what you call death, decide that the game is no longer for them or that they have learned sufficient from this game, and go on to play other games in other realities or belief systems. You are not here to get good enough to satisfy anyone else; you have chosen to master the game called life. Part of the game is that you first forget that it is a game you are playing, and you then spend time trying to remember the rules. It truly is a fun game, which is being played by tens of millions as we speak, so popular is this game called Earth!

Nothing is more important than that you should have great fun playing the game. Many of you have made hard work of this game, inventing and re-inventing rules that for the most part restrict you and do not help you win. The purpose of the game is not to please anyone else, but to be satisfied with your own achievement. The primary reason for your soul shifting to this focus is so that it can exist in a state of bliss and unconditional love despite all the 'evidence' to the contrary. The game called Earth is a challenging one, but it is far from being impossible to win.

Then who is God?

To best answer this question, let us change the 'who' to 'what', in the same way as we described the what and where we are as Omni, which makes up the 'who' of who we are. So many of you still view God as a deity that has personality, and individualised wishes and intentions. If we view the Universe as being consciousness and that you, we, and all of 'it' and 'us' and 'them' exist within that consciousness, we could more accurately describe God as being the field of unifying consciousness that binds us all together.

At the very highest levels of consciousness, there are beings that would appear from your perspective to be Gods, for they are vast, and in their vastness it would appear that they encompass you and all that you can perceive, for they are expressions of unity consciousness. These beings, and that which resides beyond them, the All-That-Is, the Source-of-All-Life, have no personal wish for you other than that you experience who you are fully, just as they can experience you and themselves through the vastness of their consciousness. There is no individual being called God, for each of us is an individualised expression of that whole and we carry within us the same qualities of the divine. You, like us, are creators, for you exist within the mind of God and tap directly into that consciousness in every moment of your existence, whether or not you acknowledge it.

So, basically, you are saying that there is no God, no creator, and that no one is in charge of the Universe?

If you wish to put it that way, then yes. But there is a God in charge in your world; there is a creator who creates in your world, and it is you!

> *"There is a creator who creates in your world, and it is you!"*

From your limited perception, you have observed your world and have made decisions about that which is higher and lower. You have decided that an ant is less than a butterfly, and a butterfly is less than a bird, and a bird is less than a dog and a horse, and a horse is less than you are. Therefore, you seek that which is 'higher' or better than you are and have created a God in 'your image'. You focus on hierarchy, and therefore create it by virtue of your focus on it, and then you look at the Universe from that perspective. So much so that you arrive on the moon or you gaze at Mars and you declare, "There is no life here," for you are looking only within your focus. I can assure you that both the Moon and Mars and all the other planets are teeming with life. It is simply that they are playing a different game with different rules. True, there is no one playing your particular game at this time on these planets, but they have done so in the 'past' and they will in the future. For now, they remain invisible, as invisible as the God you are seeking.

The experience of God comes when you experience yourself as one with All-That-Is. With this realisation, you then come to experience yourself as God, to know yourself as God. That is the game you are playing; it is the game we are playing. It is simply that your starting point in this game is the physical reality called Earth. There are many games, but all lead to the final destination. Perhaps in time we will all decide upon another destination, one that has yet to be conceived!

Who are these other 'gods' you have spoken of?

There is only one God in the terms we are speaking of; there is only one All-That-Is. However, there are those beings that are collective in nature like myself who are vast in their sphere of influence. So vast that they contain within themselves entire worlds and systems which they cradle and oversee. In this way, you could see these beings as being Creator Gods who shepherd all players in a particular game.

For example, each stellar and planetary body is ensouled in the same way you are. Your Earth has a soul as do your Sun and all other planets in your solar system. And just as you are the steward for your physical body, these beings are the stewards for their physical bodies, the Sun and the Earth. Each night as you look up at the sky and see the stars, you are in all truth viewing the physical body of a vast spiritual being. Just as you are a spiritual being focused in a physical body, these are spiritual beings focused in a stellar body.

There are indeed beings of greater magnitude than this, beings that embody entire galaxies, entire systems. These too can be considered gods for they manifest your playground within themselves. You are not separate from these beings, for it is your individual consciousness grouped together with all others within a particular game that forms the God you see. So when we speak of Higher Will, we speak of a will that works for the greater good of all.

There is no hierarchy in the sense that there is someone who is 'more' in charge than you, or who can decide who and what you may be. But there is a sense of hierarchy when we look at levels of conscious development. Even this concept is false if we consider that these higher beings are actually you, expressed at a higher level. For you are the physical extension of a non-physical being, and that non-physical being is multidimensional in nature. Just as there are some of you who have a sense that you have been in physical form before in some 'past' life, and most of you are hoping that you will exist after the demise of your current physical body, there are a few of you who understand that you exist in the highest levels of the hierarchy at the same time as you are in the physical mode. You are unaware of this, for the most part, for you are focused within the physical and believe the physical to be the most real thing. With that belief, you have difficulty in perceiving that which is non-physical, and that it is the non-physical part of yourself that actually contains and surrounds your physical body.

These gods do not rule you; they shepherd you. They do not seek to be worshiped or obeyed; they seek to hold a vision of your greater self. They spend their time telepathically transmitting to humanity a vision of what you can become. They transmit to you a vision of love, health and well-being, abundance, and the knowledge that you are creator. They transmit to you

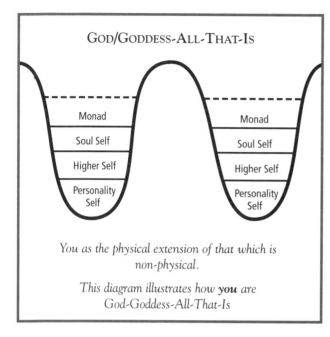

GOD/GODDESS-ALL-THAT-IS

Monad

Soul Self

Higher Self

Personality Self

Monad

Soul Self

Higher Self

Personality Self

You as the physical extension of that which is non-physical.

This diagram illustrates how **you** *are God-Goddess-All-That-Is*

Personality Self: The you that you identify with on the physical plane.

Higher Self: The Personality Self as aligned with the purpose and perspective of the Soul.

Soul Self: The eternal part of you that spans all of your lifetime experiences, both physical and non-physical.

Monad: The point at which you individuate as something other than "All-That-Is". The point where 'you' or 'I' emerges from "God".

thoughts of peace, of prosperity, of your greatness; they only seek your higher good and expect nothing in return. Why do they expect nothing in return? Because from their perspective, you are part of them, you live within them, you are them.

What we, Omni, seek is cooperation with these 'gods' and have formed agreements with them so that we may pierce the veils of the 'game' and transmit to you the teachings of oneness, of love, and of greatness. We come forth to remind you that you are gods. We come forth to remind you of the game and to assist you in reaching upwards towards your highest dreams and visions of yourselves. For just as humanity is capable of the most horrendous nightmares, each of you is capable of creating miracles and each of you has an unending capacity for love. We come not to save you, for you do not need saving. We come not to change your world for you, for you are more than capable of that, but we come as a friend to remind you of your true nature and to remind you that you are so very, very precious.

If we could transmit to you just one percent of God's pure love for you, you would never doubt yourselves again; you would flourish in greatness, each breath touched by a miracle, each winking of the eye expressed in greatness. And why do you not see us, why do you not see yourselves for who you truly are? You have convinced yourselves that you are unworthy, and in this perceived unworthiness, you treat one another as unworthy beings, and in turn, you feel even less worthy, and so you treat another as less worthy yet, and so the circle goes on and on. However, there is a crack that is ever widening, which has appeared in the consciousness of humanity. You have yearned to know who you are, you have reached out and have asked for answers. You have asked for love, and so we came, not to be worshipped, but to say that we are you, and that you are the gods!

Chapter 2

Universal Laws

Are there any laws governing the Universe?

Yes, but not in the sense that a lawmaker has devised a law. Laws exist which are natural laws, similar to the Laws of Physics that your scientists recognise. The primary law is the Law of Love; all things exist within this law and are created out of it. Love is the total and complete acceptance of what is. Love allows. Love is about allowing yourself to be who and what you are and allowing that same right to all others. Without the Law of Love, free will could not exist, for free will is free will. It cannot and does not come in portions, for you either have it or you do not have it. The Universe is a place of creation; it is a place of experience. And you have come to this world by choice to experience yourself just as you have done in many other worlds and will do again in many other worlds after this one, whether they be physical or non-physical. As a creator through experience, you have complete free will to create what you wish, and you create through the process of magnetism, the process of attraction, which is the second law, the Law of Attraction, or the Law of Increase, whichever term communicates this concept to you more strongly.

The Law of Attraction states that all that is like unto itself will be drawn to it. In other words, all things similar in nature will naturally gravitate to one another and magnetise one another into their own field. This applies to all things in the Universe; it applies to thought. All energy, and thought is energy, is magnetic to those things with a similar vibration.

> *"The Law of Attraction states that*
> *all that is like unto itself will be drawn to it."*

It is through the utilisation of this law that you have come forth into this and many other worlds in order to experience yourself. For as you experience your world unfolding around you, you are experiencing yourself, for your world unfolds in accordance with your thinking. Quite literally, what you think is what you get, and what you think is what you are. So many of you are so convinced that life just happens to you and that things impose themselves upon you that you have built whole societies and cultures upon this premise. As you are the centre of your Universe, you are the creator of it, not of some of it, not of most of it, but all of it.

See the Universe as being a large hollow sphere. It does not matter where you stand on the surface of this sphere, you will always be at its centre, and so it is with you. All emanates from you, for you are a magnet, drawing experience unto yourself so that you may know yourself in this particular experience. This is why it generally takes the average human being several lifetimes, even hundreds of lifetimes, to master this game called Earth. The reality that you have created for yourself is so convincing that it appears that there is nothing else and that you are merely a collection of gases, chemicals, and water drawn together to form a planet and your physical apparatus, your body. However, I would offer to you that even the body you have created, every last cell, every contour, every hair, is an expression of who you are, an expression of your consciousness.

The Law of Attraction does not simply disappear in the physical world; it is as active there as anywhere else in the Universe. At another time we will offer ways for you to consciously utilise this law.

What is Karma? How does it work? Many have told us that we suffer or pay back in this lifetime for what we did in a past last time.

This belief in Karma could not be further from the truth. It is not a law designed to punish you or to bring you into balance as some may have suggested, but it is merely the Law of Attraction expressed in different terms and interpreted through religious structures that for many millennia have been based on the concept of redemption.

Many teach that, if you abused your wealth in one lifetime, you will be poor in this one, or if you murdered in your last lifetime, you will suffer in this one. This is only true if you don't change your mind! What we mean is: The Universe springs forth from thought, and all action is *preceded* by thought. It is a thought that has led one to steal, abuse, or murder. So what are the thoughts of the robber? Clearly this individual does not understand the Law of Attraction, does not understand that he or she is God, does not understand the infinite love of God, and does not believe in his or her own ability to create wealth.

Your experience on Earth is not one lifetime after the next, it is one total physical experience and it is one physical experience that has many forms. Therefore, if you hold the belief in one lifetime that you are unable to create wealth, or are not worthy of wealth, and this belief is strong enough to motivate you to steal, then it is this *belief* that will follow you into the next episode of physical experience. It is not the *deed* that draws *karma* to you; it is the *belief* that led to the deed, and the **thought** behind the deed. As you re-enter this current life experience, you are automatically drawn to those parents who are magnetically attracted to you; you are drawn to them through the process of resonance. You will be drawn to parents who share similar beliefs and *experiences* concerning wealth, therefore setting up a similar pattern, until **you** decide that this no longer serves you.

However, you may make an agreement with the soul whom you robbed that you will share an experience in an upcoming life. If, however, you change your thinking, and therefore your vibration and your magnetic attraction, it is highly unlikely that you will meet this soul, or if you do, that there will be an interaction between the two of you similar to the past life experience. In saying this, what we want to communicate to you most of all is that all the answers you seek concerning yourself are to be found in this lifetime experience, with very few exceptions. We say this, for your beliefs are in the present; you hold onto them in this current time and space. Change your beliefs, and you will change your karma!

"Change your beliefs, and you will change your karma!"

No one is obliged to suffer hardship for anything. And as difficult as it may be for many of you to hear this, there is no punishment, no judgement, no failure, no negative karma. There is only experience. In the highest sense, there is no right and wrong, nothing that can turn away the magnificence of God's love for you.

There is no judgement?

No, not in the sense that most of you think of judgement. Yes, you have teachers and advisors who guide you in making choices based upon your last lifetime. But they are not there to discipline you or to point out your faults. You decide what you are happy with, you decide what you want to create next, no one else. You are in charge. Their role is to assist you in seeing a greater vision of yourself. Part of our being has been present on what has been called the afterlife, or the astral plane, as teacher and guide to those who are offering guidance to you while you are in both the physical and in the non-physical states. Our experience tells us that humanity's belief in its inferiority is so strong that it has also become part of the consciousness of the Astral Plane. Meaning that the Astral Plane of reality that 'surrounds' the Earth is a reflection of the evolution of your entire species. Therefore, those beings who enter the Astral plane at lower vibrational levels make choices concerning future lives that are 'unnecessary' in terms of hardship, for there is still a very strong belief that suffering is necessary to reach a higher spiritual goal.

Are there any other rules that apply in the Universe?

The Law of Love and the Law of Attraction are the primary laws that govern all worlds, physical and non-physical. What we would offer also are principles. A principle tells of the nature of things, an action or a flowing of energy, more of a state of being.

The principles that we offer are the Four Principles of Creation, principles that express the very nature of God and of who you are: Love, Health and Well-Being, Abundance, and Creativity.

Universal Laws do not 'govern' you, for there is no external consciousness that has decided that you must adhere to such laws. Rather there are universal principles, somewhat like the laws of physics, that describe the nature of the Universe. The 'laws' in themselves are a description of the nature of things.

The primary Law is the Law of Love; all things that exist rest on this law. It is not that love is an action, for it is also a state of being, it is also a description of the nature of things, and it is a description of the Universe, of All-That-Is. This word, love, has been misinterpreted by many, and misunderstood by all of you at times. We would define love as the complete and total acceptance of what is; we would describe love as "allowing".

"We would define love as
the complete and total acceptance of what is."

The Universe is one vast consciousness that has subdivided itself into smaller units, and further into even smaller units. This subdivision has been for the purpose of the creation of experience, for it is through experience that the whole begins to experience itself. If you are a point of light in the centre of everything that is also a vast nothingness, you cannot know who you are unless you can view yourself from outside of yourself. Then, as you gain that perspective, you then truly learn who you are through experiencing yourself as All-That-Is whilst holding onto the experience of being singular. In order for the Universe to grow through experience, 'allowing' or love must be in place, for there cannot be any limitation to the experience. For you to experience what you are, it is also necessary for you to experience what you are not. This comparison pushes you forward, for comparison is one of the most efficient ways to assist you in deciding what you want. This comparison leads to desire, and desire is the mother of creation, for without desire, nothing would come into existence.

"Free will is the natural result of love."

You are beings of absolute and total free will. Free will is the natural result of love, for love is the total and complete acceptance of what is. As love is the very nature of the All-That-Is, it is also your deepest desire, for it acts like a magnet upon your personality. All that is not love is not natural to whom you are, and all things seek to operate according to the natural laws of the Universe. Your physical reality was created so that you may experience that which you are not. In experiencing that which you are not, you began to experience that which is not love, that which is not acceptance, that which does not allow. As a soul you began to focus yourself more deeply into the physical world; you began to associate yourself more fully and completely with physical existence. This has led you to believe that the physical you is the total you, and that this you which you know will die along with the demise of your body.

The body seemed frail and vulnerable, and initially you sought to protect the body from the elements, from cold and from heat. As you observed the animals defending their physical selves against predators, you too began to see your own body as weak and something that needed protection from predators. And so it went on, until you began to see others of your own kind as potential threats, and so the lack of 'allowing' firmly rooted itself in your psyche. This was the birth of the lack of love.

The comparison drama was in place so that you could experience love, which is total allowing, as you were drawn like magnets towards it. For love is the very nature of who you are, and even though the personality self has developed so strongly that it thinks it is the real you, it cannot dominate and prevail forever, for nothing can deny its true nature forever. Love is like a magnet, it draws you towards it, and it grows within you.

"Love is like a magnet;
it draws you towards it, and it grows within you."

As you look back at human history, you can observe that you have been gradually moving towards greater levels of allowing. This movement has become increasingly more apparent in the past 100 years and the momentum of this directional move is increasing exponentially with each passing decade.

Embedded in each of you is something we can best describe as an atom. This atom holds within it your will to love. You have this will to love, for that is the very nature of the Universe. Love is the prime quality of universal consciousness, so there is not a consciousness that does not have this atom. Your will to love draws you automatically towards the state of love, of allowing. You cannot deny this will to love, you cannot resist it and you cannot flee from it, although you can pretend that you don't have it, and indeed act as if it were not there. You may even fully experience a reality or a range of feelings that may seem to be devoid of love. This atom, however faint it may appear, is within you, and is magnetic to the greater expression of love, universal love, the love of God. It is this will to love that draws you forward in your development; it is what stimulates you to growth through your many incarnations, and from one cycle to another.

This is the game of the Universe; you have decided that you want to experience many different ways of going home to love, of returning to love. This is why you embark upon new cycles and new adventures. Just as you have had many lives on planet Earth, you have completed this entire cycle from 'lovelessness' to unconditional love in many forms, on many worlds, each one adding to your experience and knowledge of total and complete love. The Universe seeks to experience itself in love in all its forms. In order to do this, the Universe holds within it the experience of "not love", the experience of darkness, the experience of separation, all for the sake of love.

With this atom within you, it does not matter how far into the 'darkness' you go, you will always eventually be drawn home to love. This is a given, it is not any other way, and cannot be any other way. As love is the very nature of God, and as all exists within the mind and being of God, then all within it is of God, and therefore is of love. This is the highest truth. All is love. All action, all beings, all things are love, for that is the foundation of all creation.

"This is the highest truth. All is love.
All action, all beings, all things are love, for that is the
foundation of all creation."

Tell us more about the Four Principles of Creation and how we can align ourselves with them?

The Four Principles of Creation are a description of your Divine nature; they are who you are. They are summarized thus:

LOVE: Love is your greatest longing. You seek to accept and allow. The Universe, or that unifying field of consciousness that you have come to call God, is a benevolent place that operates with equality and fairness, and operates according to universal laws. Love is the complete and total acceptance of what is: it is allowing—allowing all others to be who they are, and allowing yourself to be who you are. You are a being of free will, and as such, you are held in a place of total acceptance and allowing. You are dearly loved! By beginning to know that you are loved and accepted beyond all measure, you can begin to master the Universal Laws to create the life you want.

HEALTH AND WELL-BEING: Health and well-being are your natural states of being. Illness and disease are the result of mass beliefs, or individual beliefs, and the resulting fears that block emotional flow. The original fear that humans carry deep within is the fear that they are separated from their Source and are ultimately alone. Through understanding that your fears are simply that, fears, not reality, you can free yourself from the original cause of illness and disease.

ABUNDANCE: Part of your life's purpose is to move beyond lack, scarcity, and limitation. Although the experience of lack can be valuable in terms of learning certain lessons at certain times, it is not required as a learning tool. Poverty, lack, and scarcity stem directly from your primal fear, the fear that you are separated from your Source. You are the source of your own abundance. Through uncovering your beliefs concerning lack and scarcity, you can begin to create abundance in every area of your life, including financial freedom.

CREATIVITY: Creativity is at the very core of each soul, each person. You are driven to create experience. Creativity is also part of your service to the greater whole. As you create, you discover more of who you are through observing your creation. It is the very nature of the soul to be creative, but many of you have forgotten your creativity by believing that the ways in which you can express yourselves are limited to certain jobs, roles, and functions in life.

The Four Principles of Creation describe in essence who you are. They cannot be gained, earned, or awarded to you. They are the governing principles of all life. It is for you to remember that this is who you truly are. Each one of you desires these things, desires to express yourself in these ways, to live a life filled with love, to experience health and well-being, and abundance, and to create freely. Your soul's purpose, in choosing to come into the physical mode, was to manifest itself through you in harmony with the four principles.

As a non-physical being, you exist in perfect harmony with these four principles. You are a vast being, a being of vast consciousness. You are already a master of many dimensions, of many realities. Beyond the physical world, the energies are lighter, more malleable, of a higher frequency. As you adventured into consciousness, building different worlds for yourself, you developed and mastered many skills. The non-physical world from which you originated is devoid of fear. That does not mean that fear does not exist in the non-physical, for certainly it does. But beyond the astral plane, there are many planes of light. In these planes of light you have existed forever. In these realms of light, you discovered and played with your creative abilities. You played with colour, with vibration, creating many forms and scenarios in which to discover yourself. You are creator, and it is through that which you create that you learn to know yourself.

As you are such action-oriented beings, we seek to offer you tools that can enhance the emergence of these principles in your life. The tools are Self-

Appreciation, Allowing, Gratitude, and Forgiveness. Each tool has equal importance; no one tool is more important that the other. To assist you in remembering who you truly are, we encourage you to begin the daily conscious practice of these qualities, meditating upon them, writing things down. When you write things down, you bring into form a thought or an idea. This is the first step in manifesting the subject of your attention, making it real for you.

The Four Keys to Happiness

SELF APPRECIATION: Enhances your ability to create through the acknowledgment of your gifts.

ALLOWING: Is the key to living a life full of love.

GRATITUDE: Makes you magnetic to abundance. What you focus on, increases.

FORGIVENESS: Leads to health and well-being. If you are unwell, there is always something to forgive. Forgiveness is remembering the truth of who you are.

Can you tell us more about the Law of Attraction?

We have already shared with you that you are the physical extension of a non-physical being, and as such you are tapped into the same pure God force energy that creates worlds. The Four Principles of Creation are qualities that are a part of you, but at the same time they are qualities that you inherently strive towards. The reason for your striving is that you have forgotten that you are a soul having a human experience, and instead hold the illusion that you are only the you that you experience on the Earth plane. The greater part of yourself, your Inner Being, your soul, has prescribed an intention to master Earth life. Mastering the Earth experience entails moving beyond fear and living an abundant life of great joy.

Thought is the basis of all creation. Everything was thought into existence. Even those physical things made by others were first born in thought before they became matter. The fourth principle is the principle of creativity. You are the creator of your experience, and it is your thinking that creates how you experience life. Energy follows thought, and matter is energy condensed. Therefore, everything in the world of matter is a result of thought. Your entire world, the world you see as being real and very alive, is energy that has been condensed into form by thought. It is as real as you wish to make it. Collectively, humanity and others species have created this reality, this dimension of existence, in order to create another unique experience. This is the experience you call Earth. Each and every one of you has the power to create whatever it is that you are wanting through what you are thinking. All energy follows thought, and as matter is energy, it too will follow thought. The speed at which things follow thought on the Earth plane depends on your focus, skill, and practice. It does not matter how many negative thoughts you may have had in the past; it is the thoughts you are thinking right now that have the power.

The Law of Attraction states that everything draws to itself that which is like itself. In other words, all things draw to themselves that which is similar or identical. Energies of a similar nature will always be drawn towards each other; that is the principle of magnetism. All thought attracts, and thoughts attract other thoughts of a similar nature until they begin to compound and gather momentum, eventually leading to the manifestation of something very 'real' in your experience.

You are using the Law of Attraction all of the time. There is not one moment when you are not using this law. It does not need for you to be conscious of it in order for you to experience its results. Every experience, every object, every person in your life is present in your life because you have drawn them into your experience. There are no exceptions to this rule, no chance meetings, no coincidences, no accidents, no divine intervention, no external forces stopping you from having what you want, and no one rewarding you. Your experience is all created by you, you are responsible for all of it, not just some of it, or most of it, but all of it. We hear you say, "But I did not want this circumstance to come into my life." And we would agree that there are many things that you would indeed not purposefully invite into your life. Once you come to understand the Law of Attraction, you will begin to understand that whatever you direct your attention to is invited into your experience. You will also begin to know that there is no difference between negative attention and positive attention.

Your intention is sufficient to create, attract, and invite. Once you realise this law, you can choose to react in one of two ways. You can either see yourself as a victim of your own limited and fearful thinking, or you can celebrate the knowledge that you *can* have whatever you want and that you indeed have all the power you need to create it. This knowledge is a great source of freedom, for you no longer need to look outside yourself for that which you desire. No longer do you need to seek permission, either consciously or subconsciously, because knowing that the four principles are part of who you are, you can surely know that there is no higher authority in your life than you. You are it! The buck stops with you. In fact, it begins there, too. You are the sculptor, and your life is your sculpture. You are the artist, and your life is your canvas. You are the playwright, and your life is your script. So what scene are you going to write for yourself next?

Everything you have in your life can be traced back to an idea or belief. This applies equally to those things you consider to be positive and those you consider to be negative. In truth, there is no positive or negative, right or wrong, good or bad. There is only experience. Your primary motivation for coming to this planet was to master the experience of life on Earth. Therefore, all experience is valid. It is your interpretation of the experience that makes for happiness, or otherwise. You can choose to see yourself as a victim of circumstances or you can choose to reframe the negative into the positive and learn from your creations. As you begin to learn from your creations, you begin to define more clearly what you want, and as you do this, you begin to focus more clearly on your goals and desires. Then that which you long for begins to come into your life much more rapidly, because your attention has shifted away from that which you do not want towards that which you do want.

Thoughts are energy, and like all energy, attract similar energies unto themselves. This is the principle of resonance. That which you think of has a corresponding resonance, or energy match, with many objects and circumstances. As the entire Universe is energy, including the matter that makes up this book, this principle applies to circumstances, material objects, and people. Your unique way of viewing the world will affect the way in which you experience it, as well as affecting the things and people that manifest in your life. For example, if you consider money to be a great source of freedom and you feel very free to express yourself, free to be who you are, then you will automatically draw more money into your experience because there is a vibrational match between the object, in this case money, and what you think and believe.

To understand this law more fully, you need to understand that the creative energy that is at your infinite disposal is completely neutral. We have said that you are the physical extension of a non-physical being, and that being, rather than being a raindrop that has sprung forth from the rain cloud of God, is an extension of All-That-Is that has projected itself into physical reality. As this extension, you are tapped into the unlimited source of life force energy, the same energy that created the physical Universe in which you have placed yourself, the same energy that is used to create all

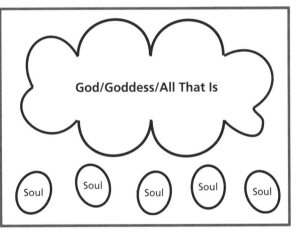

This common raincloud view of the soul's relationship to 'God' solidifies the viewpoint that we are separate whilst in the physical. Review diagram on page 18 for clarification.

that you see in your reality. This energy could not be anything other than neutral because it allows itself to be formed and moulded by your thoughts. As this energy is neutral and because it is moulded by your thoughts, it does not know the difference between what you want and what you do not want. Because you have been given free will and you exist in a Universe of free will and choice, this energy, which is the All-That-Is, can only, and will only, be formed by what you are thinking. So when you want to attract something into your life and you do nothing but think of the lack of that thing, then the Universe can do nothing but bring you more of what you are thinking, more lack of the very thing that you say that you want. The Universe does not judge whether or not what you want is good or bad; it simply is, and it responds to your every thought, to your every whim. This life force energy does not understand the difference between 'want' and 'don't want'. It only follows and supports thought. Energy follows thought, not the other way around. So as your thoughts are focused on what you fear, or things you do not want, or are displeasing to you, the ever faithful life force energy of the Universe, that very same energy that creates worlds, accurately follows your thoughts to bring into your experience that to which you have directed your attention.

Understanding this, you will begin to see that each thing you can think of is rather like a coin. It has two sides. On the one side you have the having of the thing, and on the other side you have the not having of the thing. As far as Life Force Energy is concerned, there is no difference between having cancer and not having cancer. There is no difference between having money and not having money, love and not love, etc.

Money is a great example to illustrate this point. With modern banking and computers, you calculate the amount of your money and your experience in having money in more ways than just the amount of currency notes and coins in your wallet. Your money has largely become a set of figures. Your employers transfer money directly into your bank account or your clients give you a cheque. All these things are still money, but not the currency itself, they are simply things that represent the currency. When you receive your bank statement, it can come in two forms; it can have a positive balance or a negative balance. If you have a negative balance and you now owe the bank   1,000, it is still money, is it not? You simply have a balance of 'not   1,000'. This example makes it easier to grasp this universal experience, because most of you see an empty wallet as simply being empty; "there is no money". But having a bank account 'in the red' illustrates that not only does money exist, but 'no money' exists as well, and that both things are still money.

So when you do your thinking and imagining, align your thinking in accordance with what you want to draw into your life. If you focus on the lack of anything, anything at all, you will get it. If you fear ill health, you will attract ill health. If you fear loneliness, you will attract loneliness. The Universe is not only totally equitable, it does not judge or make decisions on your behalf. You are in charge, you are the boss, the king pin, the ruler of your own experience, and the Universe cannot, and will not, do anything contrary to that unalterable fact.

Without this neutral response from the Universe you would not have true free will. So which is it? Do you have free will or do you not? It cannot be both. You cannot be both the creator of your destiny and simultaneously subject to the will of another. The one defies the other. Free will is the basis upon which there is growth, evolution, and experience in the Universe. Without it, all future would be predetermined and every soul would merely be a puppet in a grand theatre. It is our intention to help you know that you may have what you want, and do what you want, and be who you want to be. You have extended yourself into physical reality not to prove yourself worthy of a higher authority, but to add to your uniqueness and beingness through the experience of creating in this reality.

On the Earth plane, because matter is dense, and the vibrational rate of energy is somewhat slower, you experience that things come to you in a way that seems delayed. Most people, just as they have launched a new thought about what they want, within a few days begin to think about something different. The Universe responds to you instantly, yes, instantly, and as you think about what you want, it begins to immediately bring it to you. However, it seems that the majority of you change your mind on a regular basis, so the Universe receives as many order cancellations as it does orders!

The main reason, in fact, just about the only reason that your desires do not manifest instantly when you want them to, even as you think about them, is because of the other thoughts you are also offering. It all comes down to the balance of your thinking. The Life Force Energy cannot do anything but follow the thoughts you are having. Offer a thought concerning the lack of money, and that is what you will get. Offer a thought concerning an abundance of money, and that is what you will get. The same applies to love, health, and every aspect of your life. So when you look at your life and you see a lack of love or experience a lack of money or experience a lack of health, it has been the balance of your thinking concerning those subjects that has created the current circumstances. If it is love that you want more of, then your life will reflect that want accurately and proportionately according to the balance of your thinking.

So if your thoughts have been more towards the 'not having' of the thing you want, then that is what you will get. If your thoughts have been more towards the 'having' side of what you want, then that is what you will get. Each circumstance in your life accurately reflects the balance of your thinking. It cannot be any other way, for without this accurate command of Life Force Energy, you would not have free will. And as you are a being of free will, the very creative powers that you assign to God are at your fingertips. It is merely a question of adjusting the balance of your thinking towards the 'having' of what you want and you will have it. As you think more and more in terms of having, you will tip the balance of your energy into the 'having' state, and away from the 'not having' or lacking state.

As this happens, the Law of Attraction begins to work for you repeatedly. As you arrive at a greater state of 'having', you will begin to attract more of this experience to yourself, and the more you attract, the more you will attract, and so on and so on, until you move away from the experience of scarcity altogether. You then begin to realise through your experience that you are indeed God, that you are indeed creator, and that you do indeed have the command of the Universe at your fingertips, and that nothing can stop you from having what you want except your very own thoughts on the subject. As you think, so it is. It cannot be any other way; it is law.

Forgiveness seems so difficult for many of us. What do we need to understand about it in order to make it easier?

Forgiveness is remembering the truth of who you really are. The act of forgiveness is not about saying that what the other person did or said is OK. It is truly about remembering who you are. So many of you put so much energy into resisting the things that you do not want, you forget that you are indeed creator. There is nothing outside yourself that can exert itself against you. Everything that is in your experience is there because you have directed attention to it. If you remember the times when you have been hurt, and you remember and talk about that hurt, then more of the same pain will be delivered to you. If you remember betrayal, then more will be delivered to you. If you remember abandonment, then more will be delivered to you.

That which you think creates your experience of life. Yes, we hear you when you say, "But I was hurt, I was abandoned, and I was betrayed. How can I deny that?" And we say to you that you are creator and once you acknowledge that you drew these experiences to yourself, then you can also know that you have the undeniable power to draw new, more fulfilling, joyful experiences to yourself. For as you think, so you experience. Think about failure, it will be yours. Think about pain, it will be yours. Think about betrayal, and it will be yours.

When you are unable to forgive another, what you are doing is denying your own power, your own power as creator, and handing it over to that person. What you are saying is that you are subject to the will of another, to the actions and words of another, and that you have no will of your own. In reality, you are a powerful being, an eternal soul who has been given the free will and unlimited power to create what you want.

When you are unable to forgive, it means that you have denied the truth of who you really are. It is not those who have acted against you who have changed the truth of who you are. You have allowed their actions to tell you that you are something other than a powerful child of the divine.

Once you remember who you truly are, then forgiveness will become second nature, for you will truly understand that nothing can exert itself against you, that the only things that come to you are those things that you yourself have drawn in through your thinking. In knowing this, you will also know that you have a choice—a choice as to how you are going to think, what you are going to believe about yourself, a choice whether or not you will love and accept and acknowledge yourself.

Forgiveness is about remembering who you are. If you have not forgiven, then you have not remembered that you are loved beyond all measure.

Chapter 3

How Can We Stop Judging?

It seems that every spiritual philosophy teaches us about non-judgement and yet that seems to be the most difficult thing for us.

How can we stop judging, and why do we do it?

The Law of Love is the basis of all creation and of your existence, and is the very essence of the unifying field of consciousness called God. The very purpose of life is to create. The nature of God is to create. Your very nature is to be a creative being, and it is through your creations that you gain a deeper, broader, and more fulfilling experience of who you really are. It has been said that "God is Love" and therefore everything that defines what love is must also be the nature of God. We would define love as being *the total and complete acceptance of what is.*

> *"We would define love as being the total and complete acceptance of what is."*

Is it not so that, when you love someone or something, it is because you are accepting that person or thing? Love is acceptance. It is permitting that which is, to be. That is what your spiritual teachers have been talking about when they refer to unconditional love. So if unconditional love is the goal of spiritually evolved beings, then acceptance and allowing are part of that evolutionary process. Not only is the Universe a fair, just, balanced and totally benevolent place, it is also totally allowing in its relationship to you.

We have already stated that Life Force Energy is moulded and commanded by your thoughts and that this energy is neutral in nature. The Universe is totally allowing and accepting of who and what you are and of who and what you wish to become. As a species you have created a God that decides what is right or wrong, a God who will either punish you or reward you for your actions. If this is so, then the God you have created for yourself cannot be a God of love. So which is it to be? You cannot have it both ways! Is God a god of love or a god that decides what you may or may not have? If this God does indeed decide what you may or may not have, then this God also disallows and refuses to accept certain things. Such a God cannot, will not, and does not love unconditionally! So which is to be? Love of course!

Many of you who are moving into greater awareness and consciousness have taken on the concept of *karma*. Karma, according to the majority view, is a system by which the 'sins of the past' are brought into balance or are paid for in the present or in a future life. It is our observation that the only difference between hell and this view of karma is the geography! Karma is not a law that was invented by God; it is, in its essence, the Law of Attraction. Energy follows thought, and action follows thought. You would not act unless there were thoughts and beliefs that had led you to that action. It is not the action that creates the *karma*; it is the thought or belief behind the action that creates the *karma* or effect. Each action has a motivating thought or belief, and beliefs are simply thoughts that have been thought over and over until they become firmly rooted in the consciousness of the individual. Therefore, the *karma* resulting from some action of yours is simply the operation of the Law of Attraction. It proves itself to you time and time again because this Law responds to the beliefs that motivated the original action.

If you consider your life circumstances to have been disadvantageous in childhood, or you feel that you are being 'punished' or are paying back *karma* owing to past life behaviour, none of this has anything to do with any of your actions in a past life. Your life circumstances are created by the Law of Attraction and this law is activated by your thinking and not by your doing. It is because you are such action-oriented beings that you ascribe so much power to your actions. It is not your action that creates worlds; it is your thinking. Thought is the mother of creation; action is the implementation of that creation, nothing more, nothing less. As you think loving thoughts, you feel loving; as you feel loving, you act in loving ways. When you assist an elderly person to step out of a bus, this action is only an act of love if your motivation was based on wanting to provide loving assistance. If your action was based on your impatience, then it was not a loving act. The act has not changed; you still helped the elderly person to get off the bus. How they experienced the act is their reality, but it is the thought behind the action that either makes it a loving act or not. In this same way, if you had burgled or murdered or had done any number of things in past lives, it is the beliefs and the thoughts that motivated your action that will set up future circumstances, not the act in itself.

The beauty of the Law of Attraction is that, as soon as you stop thinking the thoughts that are attracting the circumstances, the circumstances will stop being created. It does not matter how many times you have thought a thought or for how long you have held a belief, the moment you start thinking other thoughts, new circumstances will be drawn to you. It is also important to remember that beliefs are only thoughts that have been thought repetitively, so repetitively that they give you the illusion of being permanent and immovable.

The truth of the matter is, irrespective of what deed or crime you may have committed in a past life, it is the beliefs that you hold true now that are important. You may, for example, believe that it is your destiny to be financially poor in this lifetime because you abused power and wealth in a past lifetime. The motivation for any abuse of power is the belief in lack. Any person motivated to want power over another does not believe in his or her own power. Therefore, it is not the abuse that has created the experience of poverty in this lifetime; it is the belief in powerlessness. Money represents freedom and personal power to very many of you, so you can clearly see how these beliefs in lack that motivated past life actions have manifested yet again in the present life—not to pay back a debt, but to give you an opportunity to re-create yourself with a different set of beliefs.

Through seeing *karma* in this way, you can truly understand that the Universe is a benevolent place and that it is indeed neutral. In this neutrality there is the experience of acceptance, the experience of allowing, the experience of Love. It is with this thought that we can say to you from a position of absolute knowing that God is love. It is also from this position of absolute knowing that we can say to you that you may do, become, or have whatever you want. And from this position of absolute knowing and of absolute love, we can say to you that you need not be, say, do, or become anything in order to win the love of God, for it cannot be won. It simply is! It is the natural state of God and, as such, it is your natural state. Love is your natural state for you are loved and you are love. It is as simple as that. Love is not complicated, it is not a secret to be found, and it is not a Holy Grail for which you must search and find; it is within you, a part of you, and it is what created you!

As most of you do not fully understand that you are the creator of your own experience and the attractor of circumstances, you have developed the habit of resisting or disallowing what you do not like. If you were to put as much energy into thinking about what you want instead of resisting, fearing, and guarding against that which you fear, disapprove of, or simply do not want, your life circumstances would be a thousand times more aligned with what you want. The opposite of love is disallowing and that is all about resisting. When you resist, you shut down the flow of Life Force Energy coming to you and that in turn lessens your ability to attract any great quantity of what you want in into your life.

What we are talking about here is non-judgement. Many of you have heard about non-judgement and have come to view it as a desirable spiritual state. The difficulty has been that you have aspired to be in a state of non-judgement because it is the 'spiritual' thing to do. If you had understood that the spiritual teachers were really talking about applying the Law of Attraction with love and allowing, you would have understood better that your judgement is based on the belief that others can affect your experience. In other words, your judgement or resistance is an expression of your not knowing that you are the creator. For as we can say to you with absolute authority that you create your own experience, we can also say to you that no one else can influence your reality unless you have drawn him or her into your experience!

Before going on to a deeper discussion of resistance, let us look at judgement. We have already established that love is allowing. We can also say that you are the creator of your own experience. As such, you are the centre of your own unique Universe, for you have created all that surrounds you and all the circumstances in your life. Therefore, everything that appears to be external to you originated from within you, for everything in your experience was attracted to you by your thinking, desires, and attention. On this basis we can say to you with absolute certainty that what you disallow or disapprove of in your world has everything to do with you and nothing to do with 'it' or 'them'. When you apply the Law of Love, it leads to absolute freedom.

> "When you apply the Law of Love,
> it leads to absolute freedom."

We can say this with certainty because love, or allowing, says: "I am what I am and whilst I am who I am, I allow others to be who they are." In moving into the state of allowing, of love, you literally begin to detach yourself from your current perceptions of who you think you are and see a broader, more encompassing, multi-levelled view of who you truly are. You begin to see the truth not only of who you are, but also of who everyone else is. The more open your heart becomes, the more allowing you become, the more loving you become; and as you become more of these things, the more detached you will become from the reality you perceive, and therefore the more control you will have of your reality and of your experience. This is the key to enlightenment!

Non-judgement was not taught to you as a 'very kindly' sort of quality, which you as spiritual beings must strive for. Non-judgement is an integral part of a clear understanding that you are the creator of your own reality. For when you judge, you are stating that there is right and wrong, and when you state that there is right and wrong, you state that you have no freedom of choice. When you state that you have no freedom of choice, you then say that you are not the creator, but that another must be the creator. When you make this statement, you deny your own divinity and that is why judgement takes you away from God. Not because God dislikes or disapproves of your judgement, but because you deny your very own divinity with every judgement you make! To judge others or to disallow others is to believe that they can in some way influence your experience. When you believe that others can influence your experience, it means that you need to exert energy to resist what you believe may harm you or affect you. No one can exert influence upon your experience unless you have attracted that one to you by way of the Law of Attraction. Everything you disallow in others is either something you disallow in yourself or it is linked to a belief that is limiting you in some way. Every judgement is about your lack of love for yourself and has literally nothing to do with the person or situation being judged.

Let us give you an exercise and some examples. Get a piece of paper and, without putting too much thought into it, write a list of everything you disapprove of in other people or in the world. Do not edit, tone down, or in any way mask what is really there. For if this exercise is truly to help you, you will need to be totally honest with yourself.

Once you have written your list, underline those which seem to have more energy behind them than others. Take a new piece of paper and at the top write one of the things you disapprove of in others. Then ask yourself why, and be honest about the answer. When you have this answer, ask yourself why, and continue to do this until you feel that you have reached the inner source of your judgement. Here are some examples to help you along the way:

* **I don't like dishonesty.**
  * because it shows lack of respect—*ask yourself why you feel this*
  * well, it means that they don't care about my feelings—*ask yourself why you feel this*
  * it means that they don't love me—*ask yourself what this means*
  * I am not loved

A person who experiences being loved is not affected by dishonesty. In this scenario, the dishonest person and the receiver of the dishonesty are both mirroring the same belief back to one another. Your indignation is telling the dishonest person "You don't love me; I am not loved" and the dishonest person is saying "I don't feel safe enough to tell you the truth, for you may not love me if I tell you the truth. Further, I don't feel loved; in fact, I am not loved."

Once again we can see how the Law of Attraction has brought together two people who have similar or identical beliefs in order that they may practice the Law of Love and in doing so change their own beliefs about themselves. It is as simple as that!

* **I disapprove of violence.**
  * because people shouldn't hurt others
  * because there are innocent victims involved
  * I am afraid of being hurt
  * I am powerless
  * I am a victim
  * I am alone

So which of the "I am" statements are true for you? Do you see how judgement takes you away from your Divinity? Believing that you are a victim, powerless, or alone states that the power of God is not with you or within you. It is once again a denial of who you are. Enlightened beings know that they are always safe, for they know they are the source of all that they experience and can choose their experience moment by moment.

✳ **I disapprove of prostitutes.**
- because they are morally wrong
- because I don't like lewd, overtly sexual behaviour
- It isn't right to be like that
- I am not allowed to be like that
- I am not allowed to be sexual
- I am not allowed

This example shows clearly that what you disapprove of in another has nothing to do with the other; it has everything to do with you. This is because the Law of Love says: "I am what I am and whilst I am what I am, I allow others to be who they are." If you are disapproving of another, you are clearly not being "Who You Are". Disapproval always indicates lack!

✳ **I disapprove of badly dressed people.**
- it shows a lack of self-respect
- dress is how I express my self-respect
- I can show that I am good enough through my clothes
- I need to be perfect
- If I am perfect, they will love me
- I am not lovable the way I am
- I am not loved

✳ **I don't like greedy people.**
- They are selfish
- There isn't enough to go around
- I am not able to have what I want
- I have always wanted more, but it never comes
- There isn't enough, or I am not allowed

✳ **I don't like snobs.**
- They think they are so superior
- They make me feel inferior
- I am not good enough

✳ **I don't like uneducated people.**
- because they make dangerous or stupid decisions
- I need to control
- I have no power
- I am unable

✳ **I disapprove of people who charge money for spiritual services.**
  - It makes it impure, I distrust their motives
  - Spirit should not be tarnished by money
  - Money is not to be trusted
  - Money is materialistic, materialism is separate from God
  - Matter is separate from God
  - I am separate
  - I cannot be trusted
  - I am not allowed
  - I am not worthy

The above examples show you in a very broad way the types of beliefs that are at the basis of judgements. The specific beliefs that you uncover may be quite different from the ones listed. The important thing is that you understand that all your perceptions of what is external to you are totally governed by your inner world. What you deem to be true about yourself and your relationship to the Universe will determine your relationship to all other things. Love yourself and accept yourself, and you will automatically love all things, all beings, without question, without doubt, and without second thought.

As love is the first Principle of Creation, it is also the thing by which you can measure your spiritual growth. There are many tools that are available to you, many books, much knowledge that you can gain concerning things of a spiritual nature. However, all of these things, all of the books, and all of the hours of meditation cannot compete with experience. It is not words that teach; it is experience that teaches. It is your ability to put love into practice that determines your growth, nothing else.

Love is not about being kind to people, and it is certainly not about ingratiating yourself in order to be seen to be loving. Love is about being authentic, being accepting of yourself and of others. Many of you look at the world and see it as a terrible place that has fallen from grace and is full of heartless, Godless, lost people who are causing ruin. None of this is true. It is true that most of humanity have forgotten who they are, but this was all part of the plan! Each of you has chosen to come into this physical experience in order to master creating in this dimension. In doing so, you knew in advance that you would forget, and that others would forget, and that it would probably take you some time before you would start remembering your purpose for being here.

> *"Each of you has chosen to come into this physical experience in order to master creating in this dimension."*

You did not come to Earth because you were not worthy of some 'higher' or 'better' place; you came here because your greater, all-knowing, broader, wiser self wanted the challenge! Not all souls choose this challenge. Far from it being the 'unworthy' who come to Earth, it is those very beings who have already mastered creation in other worlds who choose to come into the experience of separation in order to develop mastery. Once you are truly able to see yourself as one who has chosen to master life on Earth, you will begin also to acknowledge who those around you truly are. The more you either inwardly or outwardly acknowledge those around you for who they are, the more peace and harmony you will experience as you move into an experience of allowing, acceptance, and love. Love is part of your higher purpose. Love is the basis of all creation, and it is the first principle. Without it you cannot create your heart's desires. For as you lack love for others, you lack love for yourself, and as you lack love for yourself, you lack acceptance and allowing, and without allowing nothing can come into your life. First you must think it, then you must feel it, and then you must allow it. That is how you create. That is how worlds were created, imagined, desired, and then allowed!

Chapter 4

We Create Our Own Reality

You repeat often that we create our own reality, but how do we create what we want?

In simple terms, think of what you want and nothing else! The reason most of you do not end up creating all of the things you want is that you pay too much attention to what you lack and to past experience. You build your model of the world based upon past experience. Past experience is not only what you have experienced directly, but also what has been passed down to you by your parents and previous generations. You took on certain beliefs and inherited certain expectations. However, this is not to say that you don't have the money, the relationship, or the job you want because of your parents. You already have enough things to blame for your lack of success!

The commandment to "know thyself" is paramount in the quest for joyful living. For as you know yourself, you begin to understand your thoughts and beliefs. And what are beliefs? They are merely thoughts that have been thought many, many times. In a cultural context, there are thoughts that have been thought for many, many generations, so much so, they have become culturally ingrained. Therefore, for those of you who are seekers of joy, you need to make consistent choices about what you think. Your friends, family, churches, and others in authority may tell you that you cannot do or become a certain thing, and many of them think they are telling you these things from a position of love. They will convince you that they are trying to protect you from disappointment, or that what you want is unrealistic or impossible to achieve. Every instance of this is the Universe showing you where you need to change your beliefs.

As you begin to think about what you want, the Law of Attraction becomes active around the subject. Every aspect concerning that subject will become apparent to you, for that is where your focus is. Aspects of that focus will be reflected back to you through people and events in your life. For example, if you want a new job, then every aspect of finding and having a new job will manifest in your life. If you have doubts concerning your abilities, they will manifest through others telling you that you are not qualified to do what you want to do, or that you have set your goals too high. This is your opportunity to deal with the beliefs and transform them, not a sign for you to give up! If you have a belief that says that it is rare to get a good job which is fulfilling and rewarding and that most people struggle through life, you will need to deal with these beliefs and change them consciously and deliberately.

It is not that the Universe, as a consciousness outside of yourself, is 'sending' you these things to deal with; it is that your focus has changed. As you focus on a subject, the subject will grow. All things are energy, and a new job or career is also energy. This energy is unique to you and is an expression of all the beliefs, thoughts, and ideas you have on the subject. As you focus on 'the new job', all aspects of that 'energy' will be amplified in your life. Manifestation is one of the most rapid paths to enlightenment. It offers you many opportunities for growth and shows you who you are on many, many levels. When you think of anything you want, the Universe instantly starts bringing it to you in the way in which you think of that thing. By becoming aware of your judgements, prejudices, fears, and limited thoughts around any subject, you will learn to transform them to a higher expression.

What stops most of you from getting what you want is that when different aspects of the 'subject' come up for review, you get discouraged. There is no need for this. The wonderful thing about understanding that you create your own reality is that you can clearly see where you are placing your thoughts by what manifests in your life. However, we have noticed that many of you who acknowledge this power chastise yourselves for having done things wrong. You are never wrong; you are always right. You always get what you think of, what you believe!

As different aspects of the subject come up for review, most of you focus on the negative or lack side of the subject. Your world is a world of comparison. Comparison helps you know what you want by experiencing what you do not want. As your negative beliefs, or beliefs in lack, come up, bless them. Mentally thank those who express your inner doubts to you, for they are merely responding to your energy and are expressing that part of themselves which resonates with your inner beliefs. When others criticise you, it is because they are not supportive of themselves and are reflecting back to you the parts of yourself that do not support you. They are your mirrors, they are the other side of the coin, and you are both working with the same belief systems.

The Universe responds to your thinking. As you are in the world of comparison, each subject has two sides, the negative pole and the positive pole, or the lack of what you want and the having of what you want. So many of you, when you decide that you want something, immediately start thinking of all the reasons why it may not be possible or why you can't have it. All thought is creative, and each new thought that you have launches a new creation in your life. When you start to think of the reasons you can't have something, that also goes forth as a creation and counteracts the previous thought of creating what you want. This is how many of you get stuck.

Everything is energy and all energy is moulded by thought. In addition to thought, you have another very powerful ally, which is emotion. Thought precedes emotion, always. Those thoughts that stimulate great emotion or feeling in you are very powerful thoughts indeed, irrespective of whether they are positive or negative. Therefore, when it comes to drawing to you what you do not want, worry, dread, and fear are also powerful creators. The Universe does not understand the difference between 'want' and 'don't want'; Universal energy only responds to focus and the energy that your feelings add to that focus. From this perspective, worry becomes a process of creating more of what you don't want.

Desire is the driving force behind creation. Without it, nothing would exist. If there were no desire to write this book, it would not be in existence. If you had no desire to purchase your home, you would not be in it. If you had no desire to buy the shoes you are wearing, you would not have them. Desire is a powerful engine which drives the creative process. Your feelings are your friends. However, so many of you have become afraid of your feelings, seeing them as a weakness or as something less desirable. In fact, you are feeling beings, and it is your feelings that drive you towards making all major decisions.

Most of you have become fearful of your feelings because you are afraid of the feeling of disappointment. This feeling of disappointment stems from early childhood encounters with the adults around you. You came into the world as a fearless bundle of love and acceptance, willing to embrace all things. As you grew up, parenting became focused towards teaching you skills of survival and protection in an uncertain world. You began to understand at a very young age that love was not unconditional and that truth was not necessarily what was wanted. With these realisations, you gradually began to shut off your deepest inner feelings, for the deepest inner need you carry is the need to love. Most believe that their deepest need is to be loved, but in fact, the greatest inner drive that you have is to love, for that is the purpose that you came to fulfil in this and the many other lives which you have had.

Deep within you is a place of passion; it is located behind your solar plexus, in the deepest part of your being. Some have called this the Soul's Will to Love, others have called it the Core Star, and still others, the Seat of the Soul. We call it the Centre of Soul Desire, or the Soul's Will to Manifest Love. It makes no difference what you call it, this point of divine desire acts like a magnet, drawing you towards the realisation of love. It is this point of desire that you can use to stimulate, boost, and energise all of your manifesting. However, this centre of desire is often buried under layers of grief and disappointment.

So many of you have decided that it is impossible for you to have what you want, or that you are not worthy of it, or that it is not allowed. With these early childhood decisions, you cut yourself off from the source of creation within you. It is not that you have not been manifesting, for clearly you have. What we are talking about is your ability to manifest your dreams, to live out your aspirations, to live a life of potential instead of broken dreams that lead to broken hearts. In order for you to tap into this place of desire, you will need to overcome your fear of disappointment. When you feel that which you want, feel it more. And as you feel it more, add more feeling yet until you can see, taste, smell, and expect the thing you want. If pangs of fear come up for you, feel them too. If grief comes up for you, feel it. Feel all there is to feel. For as you tap into deeper desires, you may need to work through the layers in which you have surrounded it. Perhaps you will need to release or forgive a parent, yourself, or some other person in your life, and all that is fine. The process of manifesting is most successful when you feel passion for the thing you want. For you to feel passion, you will generally need to move through blockages to that passion. It is part of the process.

In addition to feelings, the next most important thing is to understand what it is that you want. That not only means being specific about what you want, it means getting clear on why you want it and what it is going to add to your experience and to your life. For example, you may want a new car. What does that new car mean to you? Is it safety? A sense of self-worth? Reliability? Beauty? Freedom? There are many possibilities, and only you can know what it means to you. Once you have identified the essence of what you want, begin to identify other areas in your life where this essence exists. For example, let us say that the new car or a house on the beach represent freedom to you. Once you have identified the essence as freedom, you can begin to look at your life and identify where you can easily add more freedom to your day-to-day life. The physical world is but a reflection of the inner world. Therefore, if to you a new car represents freedom, what you are really asking for is more freedom. Through making changes in your life, however minor, that allow you more freedom, you will align your energy with the essence of freedom, and therefore the things that represent freedom to you can enter your life more easily and rapidly.

The Universe is a place of energy and resonance. As you change or enhance your energy to be more aligned with what you want, the faster it will come to you. Sometimes, in this process of discovering the essence of what you want, you realise that it is not the material thing you want, but ways to experience that essence. Either way, the process has served you and will continue to serve you.

Once you have discovered what the essence of a thing is, begin to visualise it. As you visualise it, do not only tap into the essence of it, but also into your desire. Allow yourself to feel it fully and do not be afraid of any feelings that come up. If fears come up, feel them and go deeper. Eventually you will always feel your deeper inner desire, and that is always aligned with the love of your soul. When you have identified all these things and have visualised the end result, continue to think of what you want. Live it, breathe it, walk it, taste it, want it.

If there is anything in your life which you don't have and which you say you want, it is always because you have not wanted it enough. Not wanting it enough means that you have either sabotaged the process right at the start by allowing your 'logical' mind to convince you that it is isn't possible or realistic, or that you have withdrawn from wanting the thing because you do not want to risk disappointment. In other words, you are afraid to want it too much in case it doesn't come to you.

We hear you when you say that you have wanted something for years and years and you still don't have it. We understand this. However, remember that each subject has its positive aspect and its negative aspect, the having of it or the lack of it. When you look at the things that you have wanted and examine the balance of your thinking on the subject, what has that been? If you have wanted more money, where have your thoughts been? On the lack of it? If you have wanted a loving partner, where have your thoughts been? On loneliness or that lovers aren't to be trusted? If you have wanted a new exciting career, where have your thoughts been? On how others are more talented or that good luck is on their side and not yours? Each of your desires can be counterbalanced by your attention to the lack of what you want. If you want a baby, think not of infertility, but of the joys of parenthood. If you want a financial fortune, think of what you can do with it.

It is important to set aside time every day for daydreaming. Make your dreams as big and as real as possible. As you daydream, you set forth creation. The more you do it, the more real your logical mind will allow it to be. The more your mind accepts the possibility, the bigger your dreams will be and you will act accordingly. As your dreams get bigger and become more real, you move into the realm of probability, and then expectation. As you move into expectation, it is yours!

This process may take one day or several years depending on the dream. There is only one factor in the time it takes, and that is your capacity to believe in it! Some dreams unfold little by little and they do so because you are still in the process of convincing yourself either that you may have it, that it is possible, or that you are worthy of it. The dreams that take longer to unfold are the ones that are dogged by conflicting and limiting beliefs. Both individually and as a species, you hold many beliefs concerning abundance, money, good health, love, relationships, and success. Those things that require you to make changes to your inner self and the way you view yourself will take longer to manifest; it is a journey. However, it takes no more energy, thought, or emotion to create a new bicycle than it does to create a financial fortune. It is the same process. The difference is your feelings and beliefs about the subject!

So many of us are looking for our life's purpose, trying to figure out what our life's work will be. How can we know what it is?

The primary purpose of your life is to lead a life of joy. It is often a very difficult thing for you to hear this when we say it, or when we say that there is nothing more important than that you feel happy and good about yourself, yet this is the highest truth. How can we say that it is your primary purpose to live a life of joy? The statement is based on the Four Principles of Creation. The Universe is built on four undeniable, all-pervading principles, and it is these principles that you seek to manifest. Remember, they are love, health and well-being, abundance, and creativity. Which one of you can say that you don't want these things? Which of you can deny these things? You came forth into the *experiment* called physical matter to express yourself through the four principles, just as you *have already done* in many other realms of reality. You say, do you not, that the heart is the seat of love and desire? And have you not heard the expression "as above, so below"? The blood in your body, the water of life, is pumped around your body by your heart, which is made up of four chambers, each reflecting one principle; and so it is.

Confusion about one's life purpose is caused by judgement. So many of you hold on to the notion that there is an external authority somewhere, which you have created as 'God' in your minds, and that there are certain things that 'he' approves of. You make decisions about what is spiritual or not spiritual. Many of you spend your time trying to figure out what 'he' wants. The fact of the matter is, what 'God' wants is for you to be happy. That's it. You were born with free will, and from our perspective, love and freedom are one and the same thing, for without one, you cannot have the other.

Your life's purpose and your life's work are separate, but connected. Your life's purpose is that part of yourself, or that quality, that you came to evolve in this lifetime. Your life's purpose is more successfully accomplished during the process of developing and exploring your life's work, because your life's work will draw you to circumstances that are ideal for the achievement of your personal goals. Let us first deal with understanding your life's work.

Your life's work can be identified easily and straightforwardly. It is what you find great joy in doing, whatever that is. It makes no difference whether what you love to do is to fly planes, bake bread, teach, be a parent, a mechanic, an architect, or any number of things. Whatever makes you really happy is what makes you really happy.

Life's purpose is about the realisation of the thing you love to do. It is about overcoming the obstacles and challenges to manifesting your life's work. To follow your life's purpose you should steadfastly follow your joy, irrespective of what the world and others are telling you. When you do this, you are in a position to develop qualities such as determination, discernment, resourcefulness, courage, independence, acceptance, joyfulness, compassion, service, humility, and leadership. Pursuing the path of joy towards the unfolding of your life's work holds the key to developing the soul qualities you came to develop in this lifetime.

When you release your judgements about what is right and wrong, about what is more spiritual and less spiritual, you give your soul the opportunity to express itself more fully through you. This happens when you pursue your life's work, and therefore your passion and joy, without compromise. As you pursue your passion and joy, you are automatically aligning yourself with your higher purpose, that is, with your soul's purpose for being physically present in this lifetime. When this happens, you find yourself being more energised, more joyful, more loving, more patient, and able to express more compassion and patience. You simply become a lighter person to be around. As your new personality develops, more and more people will be drawn to you because they are attracted to your light, and you will be able to share with them the secret of your happiness. When you do this, you are fulfilling your greater purpose, and that greater purpose is to love.

The greater purpose for each of you is to live a life of joy. When you follow your passion and do what feels good, you are automatically loving and kind towards others. It is unhappy people who act in negative ways towards others. So many of you are dissatisfied with your lives because you limit yourselves on a daily basis. You dismiss your dreams and aspirations and believe that happiness is only for other people. Your life's purpose is to live the life you were meant to live, and for that you do not need to figure out what is appropriate or what 'God' wants you to do. You only have to follow your heart, and that is done through honouring your feelings.

Who are you not to honour your life's purpose? It is what you came to give the world. So many of you dismiss yourselves and your gifts as if they were worthless. Whether you are here to bake the tastiest cheesecake the world has ever had, be a parent to a gifted soul or to a child in need, be a doctor and a healer, or a taxi driver, it makes no difference what the form is. What counts is your love of life as you live it. For as you love life, you love people; and as you love people, you aid and assist people. You give, and you give your best. It is through giving your best when you feel your best that you create miracles, assisting others to open their hearts to greater possibilities just as you have opened your own heart. Spiritual growth is always attained through service to the One. When we speak of the One, we speak of God, the Universal Essence, All-That-Is. When you are in service to the One, you are in service to yourself; when you help others, you help yourself. You can be in service wherever you are, irrespective of your job or how you spend your time. If you are a leader of business, you can serve those who work for you by identifying their strengths and helping them to build upon them, encouraging all those who come in contact with you to have unlimited dreams, even if it means allowing them to move on into other directions.

Service to the One means knowing that all people are on a spiritual path, even if they don't know it on a conscious level. It means being prepared to *be* who you are at all costs and to put your happiness first, and encourage all others to make choices that support who they are and not necessarily what you want. Service to the One means knowing and living the words "do unto others as you would have them do unto you", for you know that as "you do to them, you do to me". It is about recognising that you are One; there is no separation, only unity. Service to the One is about coming home to who you really are. Do that which gives you joy. If you don't know what joy is, then choose that which makes you feel free, for joy, love, and freedom are the same. Set yourself free!

How do we balance working 40 hours a week to pay for our homes and bills, and also study or work towards the thing we love to do the most? Most people I know can't just give up their jobs and go and do what they love to do.

We understand you when you see yourself as stuck where you are and not able to go where you want to go. It is as simple as this. It is not the circumstance of your life that is the problem; it is your beliefs that are getting in the way. You have beliefs that say things like "all artists struggle and are poor" and an entire subculture of out-of-work actors has grown up with the belief that only very few are successful. So you decide that you want to be an actor. You go to acting school. Others tell you it will be difficult. Perhaps even parents, family, or friends will ask you if you are sure you want to live a life of struggle and poverty. After all, that is what actors do, isn't it? And there you have it; you have bought into the beliefs. These beliefs exist because those of you who are presenting your creativity to the world are presenting a particular part of yourself, and here we come to the core of the problem—self-appreciation. We tell you this from a position of absolute knowing: Success does not come from being in the right place at the right time, or knowing the right people, or necessarily from talent. It comes from two things and two things only: from an absolute desire to become the thing you want to become, and from self-appreciation.

If you could change all of your beliefs overnight concerning money, your self-worth, and your ability to earn a living by doing what you love to do, you could launch your new career tomorrow. However, because you have been told that life is difficult and you have few choices, and success is only for the lucky and the few, you believe it, and therein lies the problem. If you look at the lives of all those who are successful, you will see that many of them have made sacrifices in order to do what they love to do. It is not that the sacrifices were absolutely necessary, rather that because of the prevailing belief systems of your culture, the sacrifices were necessary for them. Desire can take a long, long time to manifest. Add a healthy dose of self-appreciation to desire, and all the obstacles will disappear.

Many of you choose safety and security over passion, and you do so because you have forgotten that all that is comes from within. You have forgotten that you are creators and that you can indeed have whatever you want. It is as simple as that. We cannot put it any other way. Many of you now believe that you create your own reality. We have said it in this book many, many times and will continue to repeat it until you really believe it. You see, you create all of it—not some, not most, but *all of it*. If there is something in your life that you want but don't have, it is because you are blocking it. We hear you and we feel your anguish, frustration, and anger when you read these words and say, "But I understand the laws of the Universe; I have wanted this and that, but they don't work for me. What am I doing wrong?" We say to you, you do nothing wrong, you are simply distracted from the truth. The truth is, you are perfect just as you are. However, we must remind you that every thought and feeling you have is creative. Think only of what you want and it will be yours.

Do you believe that you can go out and do what you love and be very successful at it and receive a good income? Probably not. Then allow your desire for it to work for you. Live your desire and make changes in your life so that you can do what you love to do, and use that time to work on your beliefs about having what you want and on self-appreciation. If you really want something, you will make sacrifices to have it. Live in a smaller home, take the bus instead of having a car, work part time—there are many options open to you.

Although you can create miracles through changing your self-image, much has been gained through the struggles you have encountered. Struggle has been the cornerstone of spiritual growth on your planet since the dawn of time. It has assisted you to develop qualities such as determination, patience, courage, compassion, and others that help you expand as beings. However, the struggle is not necessary. But if it is in your life, learn to love it. See the gifts it is bringing you and love them. Look back at all the struggle in your life, at how much you have grown, how much you have expanded, how much more wise, loving, and compassionate you have become. Do you recognise the person from all those years ago? Probably not. Until you change your beliefs, struggle will be part of your life. Make the best of it by making it your ally. Honour the struggle and scorn it no more, for it serves you well.

How can we learn self-appreciation?

You can learn self-appreciation just like any other skill you wish to learn. If you wanted to learn how to bake cakes, first you would buy a book on the subject, then perhaps ask others who have baked cakes, and then try your hand at it. When you begin to enjoy the results— eating the cake—you practice some more, and then some more, and then some more, until you become satisfied with your level of cake baking. Are we trying to say that self-appreciation is a piece of cake? Indeed we are. It is only a matter of practice.

Many of you have a deep belief that you are not worthy, so it is difficult for you to practice self-appreciation. You believe perhaps that self-appreciation is haughty, arrogant, or something to be ashamed of. Let us tell you this truth: the Buddha and the Christ got to where they are through self-appreciation. How could they do otherwise? "But they were special," we hear you say, and we reply to you, "They were once just as you are. Many lifetimes, much struggle, the same path, the same pain, the same dreams and aspirations. That is why they are your greatest teachers today, for they **know** the path and have **lived** the path. All of it!"

Self-appreciation is a matter of practice. Start today. Take a piece of paper and write down five things you love and appreciate about yourself. Do the same tomorrow, and the day after, and the day after. Each day, write down specific things for which you appreciate yourself. Make this fun; add a friend or loved one to the game. Give someone else a list of the things you love and appreciate about him or her. Make it a weekly or daily event. Practice, practice, practice.

As you become more appreciative of yourself, you are more and more open to the light, love, and inspiration of your soul. As this occurs, you are more connected to the universal mind. As this happens, you are more inspired and new ideas come to you. And guess what? You get even better at the things for which you appreciate yourself.

Perhaps you want to be a dancer, but you need to build up your skills. If you love dance, you will align vibrationally with the essence of dance. If you add self-appreciation to this, you will open up to your soul's input, for you will be open to receive. As this happens, your skills multiply, you get better and better, and consequently you appreciate yourself more and more. This is how it works. Self-appreciation is the key to all of your successes, and self-deprecation is the cause of all your failures.

How can we overcome the fear of disappointment? I have tried many things that have been unsuccessful. Now I feel like giving up and resigning myself to accept less than what I want.

As you grow in self-appreciation, you come to expect your success. This happens because, as you open to yourself through self-appreciation, you get more in the flow of the Universe, more aligned with the consciousness of your greater self, your soul. As this happens, more and more things that you want will come your way. You will be having thoughts of abundance, and as you cross the car park to your car, you will see a shiny coin on the ground. Pick it up! There are no coincidences in the Universe. The more self-appreciation you practice, the more you will transform your beliefs about having and doing and the more synchronicity will play a part in your life. As you experience more and more synchronicity, you will begin to expect that all will go well, for the Universe is handing you the evidence on a daily basis that all is well and good and going your way. Self-appreciation is the key to everything, for it is self-love, and there is no higher truth than love! When you resign yourself to having less than you want, you are deciding that you are less worthy. Is that a decision you really want to continue to make?

I am a woman in my late forties. My children have all grown up and I feel stuck. I want to know what my life's purpose is, but just don't know what I want to do. You say to us, "Do what you love to do", but I am not sure that I know what that is.

You have been a caretaker and homemaker for many years, haven't you? You are simply out of practice when it comes to asking yourself what you want. For years you have taken care of the needs of others, your children, husband, perhaps even the needs of one of your own parents. Are you surprised that you don't know what you want? How often did you express your needs and wants to others? Perhaps you did and they didn't listen. Why didn't they listen? Because you carried on doing what you normally did and they assumed that all was OK. Remember you teach people how to treat you. Do not be angry with them, or indeed with yourself. But realise that you did what you chose to do then, which was to raise a family. Now it is only a matter of making different choices and if you don't know what to choose, then your first choice is the choice to make choices. Each day as you awaken, say this little prayer or affirmation to yourself. Above all, do this **before** you start thinking of all the things you need to do. Say to yourself: "Today I will begin to see more and more of what it is I love to do. As I see it, I will acknowledge it; as I acknowledge it, I will explore it further."

You simply need to practice asking yourself what it is that you want. Don't just allow your day to happen to you, but pre-pave your day with intention. Write down all the things that interest you and then investigate, gather information and data all around you. Visit places where they do things you like, call them up, buy books on the subject, buy tapes, videos, whatever it takes for you to discover if you are on the right path. Join a local club or go to evening classes and remember, whatever obstacles come your way are merely signposts directing you towards changing your inner beliefs. If you get rejected owing to your age, then you need to look at that. If you are rejected owing to your lack of experience, then you need to work on more self-appreciation. You are never too old to have a happy childhood. Enjoy your adventure!

I am about to turn 60 and although I have been doing what I love to do, I am not sure that I want to do it any longer. I also can't imagine just doing nothing and waiting for the demise of my physical body.

If you wait for the demise of your physical body, it will be yours sooner than you bargained for, because that will be the subject of your attention.

As you reach what you experience as the closing years of your physical life, look back at all you have done. Will you be able to slip away knowing that you have done all that you wanted to and given all that you wanted to give? What do you want to leave behind as a legacy? Perhaps you have given a lot already, so what do you want to truly give to yourself? This time of your life is best used for considering the gifts you can give to yourself and others. Perhaps the gift of forgiveness to a long-lost friend, or making peace with a family member, or releasing yourself from some guilt you have held on to for far too long. This is a time for gifts. What would you like to give to the world? The gifts you leave behind pre-pave your future experience.

I am in a situation where I dislike my job, dislike my home, and have no idea what I want to do or where I want to live. Every day seems like a difficult task. How can I turn this around?

When you are in this position, you are in a position of great resistance. You are focusing so much on what you do not want, it seems as if all those things that you don't want are in control of your life. Remember, the Universe reacts to thought. Thought is the basis of all creation. Therefore, when you are in a position of great resistance, your attention is focused almost entirely on the things that you don't want. This is a very uncomfortable position indeed to be in. What you can do is shift your focus, even if it is only a small shift and for short periods of time. What most of you do when you try to be positive in such situations is try to see the situation changing into a more positive one; however, your focus is generally still on the situation. The Universe can only deliver to you that which you focus on. Instead of seeing the situation going away, simply visualise a new situation, a new job, a new home coming your way. There is a universal law that says you cannot leave anything until you love it. What that means is that, in order for something to leave your life, you must first release it by accepting it. As you accept something, you cease resisting it; as you cease resisting something, your focus is no longer on it; therefore, you are no longer giving it energy, no longer giving it life.

So many of you simply allow your life to happen to you. You have become reactive beings instead of the creative beings which is your true essence. As a reactive being, you simply allow your day or your life to unfold, not setting any particular goals, or defining your life through the perspective of your belief systems.

In such situations, where everything seems to be wrong and not as you want it to be, you can easily and simply shift your focus by making a conscious choice to do so. Intention is a strong generator of creative powers. When you intend to do or have something, it comes to you much more quickly than when you decide that something would be nice to have. Each morning as you awaken, sit up in bed and set an intention for the day. Say to yourself something like, "Today I intend to see new opportunities for making a living, and I invite and allow these new opportunities to reveal themselves to me," or "Today I intend to see all that is positive in my life." As you do this, and make these statements with *intent*, you launch a new creation in your life, for the Universe cannot do anything but respond to your statement of intention. Remember, your thoughts create your own reality, not some of it, not most of it, but all of it. If your life is full of what you do not want, then shift your focus back to what is wanted. If you do not know what you want, then simply ask the Universe to show you during your day examples of the things that give you joy.

When you find yourself in such a situation, it is your job to make consistent choices about where you place your attention. As you make this consistent choice, the Universe will respond to you in ways that will seem magical or miraculous. In fact, it is neither magic nor a miracle. It is universal law, for you are creator. What you think is what you get, what you think is what you get, what you think is what you get. Each event, person, circumstance, or thing in your life can be traced back to a belief or a series of thoughts. Although we understand that you did not say to the Universe, "Give me a job I will hate", or "Give me a home I will not like", you have been sending out feelings and thoughts that attracted this situation. For you to discover how you got what you got, simply ask yourself how you feel about the situation.

How does the situation make you feel? Trapped? Lacking in freedom? Frustrated? Powerless? If this is what you are feeling, then what beliefs do you have surrounding freedom and personal power? Through feeling what it is that you feel about any given situation, you will be able to uncover your core beliefs and thought patterns that attracted the situation in the first place. Once you know this, you can easily change your belief through giving yourself a new one, a new affirmation for life. However, you need not do any of this at all if you simply set a very strong intention to create anew. Nevertheless, in our observation of humanity, we recommend that you go to the core of the problem through feeling what it is that you feel about it. You see, feelings are a result of thought, and any feelings of powerlessness are there due to a belief that you are powerless to create what you want. Going to the core will assist you in n.......g more permanent and far deeper inner changes.

It may be that this home and this job **were** the things that you truly wanted when they first arrived, or for the first couple of years. Now you need to ask yourself what has changed. *you are evolved beings and constantly changing.* All that you want to manifest is merely a reflection of consciousness. Matter reflects consciousness and is moulded by it. As your consciousness evolves, the material things in your life will need to evolve and transform along with it. As you grow, there will be times when you wake up one morning and decide that what you have no longer fits who you are, although once it fitted wondrously.

So many of you are apt to look for safety and security, forgetting that true security comes from within. You ignore all the inner impulses that are telling you that where you are in your physical world and what you are doing are no longer a reflection of who you now are inwardly. Then it seems that all of a sudden you wake up and nothing fits any longer, and often you still do nothing, until it gets so uncomfortable you have to take action. If you would only trust your feelings and listen to those inner impulses and act upon them immediately, your life would be full of joyous and tranquil transition from one expression of the inner you to another expression of the inner you.

You see, your soul, that greater, eternal part of you, wants to fully manifest itself through you according to the four principles of creation. It communicates this to you through your emotions and feelings, and sometimes these feelings can be subtle. Essentially, when you feel good, you are on the right track. When you feel uncomfortable or bad, then you are on the track that will only give you those things you do not want. It is through good feelings that your soul inspires you to move as if riding an upward spiral; it simply gets better and better. We encourage you not to do what is logical, not to do what is 'right' or expected, but to do what feels good. For as you feel good, you radiate, and as you radiate, you draw power and energy to yourself. As you draw power and energy to yourself, you become a master creator in the physical dimension, and **this** is the reason why you are in the physical dimension. You came to create!

Chapter 5

Abundance

So many spiritual teachers talk about abundance and the importance of abundance in our lives. How can we be abundant in our physical world without harming the planet?

As we have mentioned before, abundance is one of the four principles of creation, and we will repeat this saying often until you begin to believe it. If God were an individual, who would be the wealthiest person in the Universe? God, of course, for all is contained within the mind and heart of God, and do you not seek to be at one with God? Then do you not seek, in this lifetime, to discover that you are God? You are God, one with all, because you are the physical extension of that which is non-physical, that which is pure essence, that which is God/Goddess All-That-Is. If this is so, then the abundance of the Universe is within you. It cannot be anywhere else. It cannot belong to another, or come from another; it can only come from within you. However, because you have believed yourselves to be so unworthy, you have sought to deny that you are God, and you believe that you are powerless, that you are in poverty. The true poverty of humanity is the poverty of spirit, and that isn't because you are not good enough, or not spiritual enough, it is because you deny on a daily basis that you are God. You deny your greatness; you focus on all that is limiting. The damage you are doing to the planet comes from a place of lack; it is not because you are becoming greedy in the sense that you want things that you may not have. Nonetheless, greed is the primary cause of your environmental ravages.

Greed has developed amongst you because your spiritual selves have been abandoned by your culture. You came into the world open, embracing, needing no reason to love, you simply were love. Then you began to learn about rules, what was expected, and you also began to learn that spontaneous love was neither welcomed nor encouraged. You began to feel abandoned, for the one thing that you desired most to do, that is to love, was left unacknowledged and unnurtured. This led many to feel deprived—deprived of love, deprived of recognition, and deprived of power. This sense of deprivation has made many search for power and for things that they think will fill the emptiness. This sense of deprivation can become like a hungry animal that is insatiable, always needing more and more and more just to feed itself. This is how humanity has expressed itself in the past few thousand years.

As your cultures became more structured and more rule-based, the power of political and religious authorities increased, and this meant the dimming of spirit, the clouding of the sense of who you really are, a being of love and light. As a species you have sought power to nourish yourselves, reducing this sense of deprivation, and as you have done so you have sought dominion over your environment and over all that which appears weaker. Great empires have emerged, nations have invaded one another, and you have seen yourselves as masters of the Earth instead of stewards of life on Earth. You have justified this stance in the name of some of your religions. All this has been about your search for power. As you look back on your own life, you will notice that there have been times when you have sought power over another or when you have tried to control situations. As you evolve, you begin to see that this search and hunger for power never overcome the feeling of deprivation that you carry. It is at this stage that you begin to go inward and feel out what it is that you want. You learn all about feelings and inner impulses, and you begin to ask yourself who you are. This is when you begin to see that your search for power has been destructive and in the long run has not assisted you one iota. This is the dawning of a new age for you, for you begin to seek authentic power, the power of love, and this power can only, and does only, come from within, from the God/Goddess within, from the source of all things that lives deep in the core of your being. At this stage you begin to get a faint flickering sense of why you are here, what you came to do, and you see a broader picture and begin to understand that all things are related and that indeed all things are one.

Just as you as an individual go through this journey in your life, humanity also experiences this journey collectively. Humanity has been seeking power for many millennia, and history is witness to that fact. Now you are in the midst of understanding that there is more to you than meets the eye. You are beginning to understand that what you do in one part of the world has an effect on other parts of the world. You are beginning to understand that there is one world ocean, not many oceans and seas with many different names, but one body of water that feeds and sustains all life on Earth. As you see this as a species, you begin to understand that you are one, there is no separation. As above, so below. Your environmental crises are merely reflections of your spiritual crises. You have separated yourselves in your search for power and now you are beginning to see that you have been one all along. Physical manifestations are **always** expressions of inner change, inner direction, inner intention.

The advent of the Internet and the explosion of telecommunications in recent years are testimony to the fact that you are maturing as a species. This maturation process is rapidly taking you towards unity consciousness. This we applaud and celebrate. Not because where you were in your power struggles was a bad or evil place, for you were at a normal stage of evolution, a stage that is experienced on all physical planets in all civilisations. But we celebrate you in this time of growth and opportunity because you are on a homecoming journey. You are beginning to remember who you are, you are beginning to remember who we are, you are beginning to experience the God within, and that is the homecoming we speak of.

Your relationship to the Earth has hitherto been based on lack. You have used fuels that cannot be replenished, which is a direct reflection of your consciousness. However, as you understand that you are one and are all connected, you will begin, indeed have already begun, to find new ways to harness the natural energies of the Universe. There are sufficient resources in your world to house, feed, and clothe each individual and to allow each person to live with a sense of wealth. The issue is changing your consciousness. So many of you worry that, if you tap into your natural essence of abundance and begin to manifest those physical things you desire, you may in some way harm the planet. We offer this thought to you: as you awaken to your natural sense of abundance, you add that to the consciousness of the planet and add to the transformation of the species.

Those who take, take from a place of lack. Those who act greedily do so from a place of deprivation. Your world is a place of contrasting opposites. You have the greedy who act from feelings of deprivation and seemingly prey upon those who are living in deprivation. It is not the greed that causes the lack, it is the inner feelings of **both** parties that creates the lack. It is the belief in lack and in the feeling of deprivation that creates the world situation as it is in your time.

The greatest service you can do to humanity is to move out of poverty consciousness into a consciousness that recognises that you are **one** and that abundance is your natural state.

The four principles of creation are law. They simply **are**. You cannot deny them, even though you may try very hard. And it may seem that you are succeeding in denying that you are by your very nature love, that you are by your very nature health, that you are by your very nature abundance, and that you are by your very nature a creator, that you **are** by your very nature God. Yes, you may seek to deny these things, but they cannot be denied, for you cannot deny who you are. You are God!

Above all things, you are creators. Once you understand as a species that you have the power of the Universe at your fingertips, you will use that clear understanding to create with. This will lead to a great many new inventions and different means of harnessing the energy of the sun and also universal energy, yes, energy as if it comes from nowhere at all. This universal energy is all around you. It is in you, it is in your body, in the air that you breathe, in every molecule, in every cloud, it is everywhere. Soon you will discover the means to use this infinite source of energy and power, and great good will come from this. Indeed, this knowledge and the means to create such technology already exist, but the majority of you are not yet ready to embrace such power, for when you do, you will be able to do things that are beyond your imagination. This harnessing of universal power will come about once it is understood that you are connected to all things, not before.

Just as you will not have contact with alien races until you have contact with other sentient species sharing your world, the dolphins and the whales, you will also not harness this energy en masse until you understand that you are one and understand the responsibility that goes with that. Let us be clear, it is not we, or any other beings, that stop you from discovering and harnessing this power. It is your own consciousness. Some already understand this, even within the scientific community. However, mass consciousness determines what develops for you as a species. The changes are coming, and they begin with you. Think in unlimited ways. Think rich, grow rich, and know that you are a child of the Universe and that all is well and all is happening just as it should in its proper time and place.

You see, love, power, and money are all the same thing. Money is merely the physical manifestation of love and power. We can say this for we know that authentic power stems from love, and is indeed love. So what is authentic power? Authentic power stems from allowing. When you are in the state of allowing, not only are you unaffected by external circumstances, but you allow yourself to be who you are, you allow yourself to **be** God. Often when there are feelings of deprivation, many will seek power and money as compensation for that feeling of lack; and those who seek power lack self-love and very often others have no love for them, so that both the giving and receiving of love is absent in their lives. Feelings of lack are the cause of humanity's woes, not greed in the sense that most see it, but the true underlying cause of greed.

When we are faced with financial difficulty or crisis, how can we attract money into our lives?

First, you need to understand where poverty, lack of money, and financial crises come from. We have said that love, power, and money are the same. For many, that is difficult to accept. However, money is merely the physical manifestation of the two core qualities that express who you are—beings of great power and great love. At the core of all of your experienced misfortune are two beliefs.

These beliefs are: "I am powerless" and "I am not loved". These two beliefs have become the scriptwriters for the lives that the majority of humanity experience. These beliefs are the great 'lie' or illusion beyond which you have sought to move in the physical dimension.

When you are faced with financial shortage, it always has to do with your not being in harmony with your core. At your core you wish to express your power through love. Love is the complete and total acceptance of what is; it is being in a state of allowing. If money is not flowing into your life, it means that, in one or more areas of your life, you are not in a state of allowing, not in a state of freedom, or not acknowledging your true power. If you are in a relationship that limits your freedom, you will experience either a lack of money, or anxiety concerning the money you do have. If you are in a job that you do not enjoy, then you will cut off the flow of pure creative energy, and the flow of money will be restricted.

Feelings are your friends. When there is a lack of money, it is much more efficient to feel what is going on instead of trying to figure out logically what you can do about it. The questions to ask yourself are these: Where am I lacking love or freedom in my life? Where am I restricting freedom? Am I honouring and loving myself? Where do I feel powerless? Do I feel overwhelmed in any area of my life? You will discover that in one or more areas of your life you are indeed holding onto the core beliefs of "I am not loved" or "I am powerless".

So what to do about it? First, understand that self-appreciation is the key to spiritual and personal growth. When you practice self-appreciation, your vibration increases as you align with the universal truths of, "I am love" and "I am powerful". This will automatically make you more magnetic to money.

You also need to consider your thoughts about money. Remember, that everything in your world has its opposite and that the Universe brings to you that on which you are focusing. Money can manifest in your life as the lack of money or as an abundance of money. What will manifest for you is the side of the subject that you are focusing on. If you focus on the lack of money, that is what you will get. If you focus on the having of money, that is what you will get. The Universe is very even in its delivery of everything to everyone, for you all get exactly and precisely what you are focusing on.

We understand that when you have little or no money and the bills are pouring in and you cannot see a way out, the lack seems very real to you. And the evidence suggests that what you are experiencing is real and that what we are offering to you is not realistic. However, as you remember that it is what you *feel* that makes the difference, you can use your shortage of money, or anything for that matter, to work for your benefit, for it gives you an opportunity to resolve deeper issues once and for all. If you are focusing on the lack of money, and that is what manifests, it is not actually the focus on money that has caused your lack. Remembering that money is **representative** of love and power, and your focus on the lack of money is *symptomatic* of your inner feelings of powerlessness. Yes, you can use affirmations and redirect your focus onto the having of money and initiate a change in your financial fortunes, but this is often temporary. The work that is truly required is to uncover the deeper feelings that tell you that you lack love and power.

Emotions are the result of thought; they do not spring up without there being a sponsoring thought. Somewhere along the line you have taken on the belief that you are not loved or that you lack power. From your standpoint, you may have had much evidence to show you that indeed you are not loved by some people, or by many, and that indeed in certain situations you did not have any power. However, all this evidence is merely a manifestation of the original core belief and simply reinforces that belief.

Your soul communicates with you directly moment by moment, minute by minute, in *every* waking hour. It does so through emotions and feelings. It was agreed before you came into this physical existence that your soul would guide you and assist you to achieve the goal of manifesting fully through the four principles of creation. Your soul understands that *all* thought is creative and that you have the power to create all of your reality in the physical dimension. As your soul's deepest desire is to manifest in love and to be creator, it guides you with feelings. When you have a thought that creates the opposite of your primary intention for being present on the planet, your soul will communicate this through the creation of negative emotion. So, if you think about struggle and poverty, you are going to feel bad. You feel bad when you do this because your soul **knows** and **understands** that as you ponder these subjects, you are launching them as creations in your life. As the negative feelings filter through, they are literally your soul shouting, "No! No! No! Don't think like this, this is not what *you* want!"

The opposite is also true. Have you ever sat with a friend and fantasised about winning the lottery and what you would do with all the money? As you share your dream of a large home, being able to give to charities, surrounding yourself with beautiful things, and being able to buy houses and cars for your family and friends, don't you feel good? Of course you do! You feel good because your soul is saying to you: "Yes! Yes! Yes! Think like this, be **unlimited**, acknowledge your abundance, acknowledge *me*, the God within, the source of all true wealth."

When in financial crisis, most of you focus on the problem and not the solution, which simply leads to the deepening of the crisis. When you wake up one morning and realise that your finances are on the lack side, the first thing to do is simply ask yourself how you want your finances to look. As you say to yourself, "I want to be wealthy" or "I want more money to flow more easily into my life," you immediately begin to shift your vibration into the positive aspect of money. As you make these statements, your soul recognises that you are speaking words and sending out thoughts that are in alignment with who you truly are, and therefore begins to feed you positive emotion as an encouragement. Your words and thoughts are powerful allies.

We understand that you find it difficult to think of abundance when there are accounts that cannot be paid. However, did you realise that worrying is doing exactly the opposite of what we have just suggested? Worry is simply using the laws of the Universe to create more of what you don't want in your life. So, since you are going to respond to the lack by throwing out more creative thoughts anyway, why not make them positive ones instead? We are not asking you to do anything you are not already doing. As you sit and worry, you are visualising and bringing into being things that you don't want. You are in fact showing yourself how powerful you are. Look! You have created even more of what you don't want! What a powerful being you are! What a wise being you are, for you understand the Laws of the Universe and are using them. Do you see the humour and beauty of this? You **can** focus on the positive, for just as you make the choice to focus on the negative, you can make the **choice** to focus on the positive. All your unpaid accounts are merely evidence of your ability to create! Now all you need to do is turn the dial.

As you practice asking yourself what you want, you activate the Law of Attraction. The Law of Attraction says, "That which is like unto itself will be drawn." As you think about what you want, you stimulate positive feelings, within which is the response of your Inner Self. As you begin to feel that which you want, you become magnetic to it. Each thought that you have is magnetic to all things that are similar in nature, and that starts with other similar thoughts. As you ask yourself what it is that you **do** want, you automatically align yourself with other thoughts of a similar nature. You can take advantage of this by becoming quiet and simply allowing your thoughts to grow and evolve. Within a minute or two, your thoughts would have evolved into much bigger and better dreams. We understand that the natural tendency of many people is to say, "But this is not real, it is fantasy." Let us say to you again—when you are worrying about what might happen, you are indeed doing this same exercise, but in the negative sense. You know these techniques already; you know the Laws of the Universe. It is your choice: you can worry, which is using your imagination to draw more of what you don't want into your life, or you can choose to focus only on that which you want. We hear you when you say, "But Omni, should we not face reality?" and we say to you, "Do not face reality, change it!"

For money to flow freely in your life, it must be received and spent joyfully. Whenever you resent paying a bill or paying someone for a service, you block the flow of money into your life. Often those feelings of resentment stem from your belief that the money you have is limited. You feel unwilling to give your hard-earned money away on something that does not give you joy. Each material thing that you have and each service that you pay for has an essence or quality that it brings into your life.

For example, your telephone holds within it the essence of communication. Your car or monthly rail or subway ticket holds within it the essence of travel, freedom, and mobility. Your computer, printer, and other tools you may be using hold within them the essence of communication. When you shift your perspective to see the essence behind all the things you pay for each month, you will begin to feel gratitude that they are in your life. This will lead you to pay for them with more joy. When you pay your bills with joy, in recognition of the essence which the service or thing is giving you, you open your heart to receive more abundance into your life. Gratitude is the greatest healer there is and the more you can express gratitude, the more filled with joy and abundance your life will become.

The next time you pay a bill, take a few moments to consider the essence behind what you have received. Take your telephone bill: your telephone gives you the freedom to contact friends and loved ones who may live far away. It allows you to create business opportunities with clients or prospective employers whom you cannot easily meet face to face. Your telephone represents freedom of communication. Now imagine that you don't have it, and get a sense of the gratitude you would feel if it came into your life. There are plenty of things to feel grateful for. You only need to open your eyes and heart to see them all around you.

Every day of your life, you can acknowledge all the gifts that you already have, and congratulate yourself for having created them. How many things do you have in your life that give you pleasure, for which you can feel genuine gratitude? You may be in a situation where your only feeling is one of lack, feeling that your life is going nowhere and feeling stuck financially. If you are in a financial crisis, concentrate on what you have, rather than on what you do not have. This will open your mind and heart to more opportunities for attracting money, allowing miracles, and creating room for the things that you want to come into your life. The secret to having a successful money flow in your life is to concentrate only on the things that you want. Do not give a second's thought to the things that you do not want.

Many of you, when you try to think of improving your life, begin to concentrate on what you do not want. You do not want to be poor, you do not want financial struggle, you do not want work that is dissatisfying or a boss who is domineering or unfriendly. Begin today to concentrate on what you want, because whatever you concentrate on grows, including those things that you do not want. Tell yourself a hundred times a day what you do not want, and guess what? It's yours. So change your perspective to concentrate only on what you do want, and it will be yours even more quickly. Add to that a daily practice of acknowledging what you already have, expressing gratitude for it, either mentally or verbally, and you will soon be on your way to creating all the things you have ever dreamed of. Be patient with yourself. Many of the thought patterns in your society are based on the negative, on what is not right and what must be improved.

Many conversations on subways, in restaurants, and in workplace cafeterias are based on what is wrong, who is doing what to whom, and what is wrong about it. Stop! You can choose to withdraw from such conversations or turn them around so that the emphasis is on what is positive. Offer an idea about what positive steps can be taken to create change for the greater good of all. As negatively oriented conversation is so deeply rooted in your society, it may be difficult for you to rise above those thought forms and behaviour patterns overnight. One positive thought that is backed up by a strong feeling can cancel out thousands of thoughts of a less positive nature. You will need to be patient and forgiving towards yourself. Train yourself on a day-to-day basis to choose positive thoughts that include gratitude—thoughts that tell you why you can have what you want, instead of believing those thoughts or people who tell you why you cannot have something you desire.

All thought is choice. Some thought forms are so commonplace they may not seem like a choice. Many of your thoughts concerning money, wealth, and abundance are beliefs that you took on in early childhood. You were not taught to question such beliefs. You simply accepted them as truth because that is what everyone around you believed. It is still a choice to believe them and to hold on to them. Even thoughts that you have had a million times over can be changed in a relatively short period of time. With dedication and focus on your goal, you can create all the abundance you desire, irrespective of the local economy or what other people around you may be telling you.

I live in a city where there are many poor people, often homeless, and many of them beg on the streets and at traffic lights. As a spiritual person who cares about the planet, I am often lost as to what to do. On the one hand, I believe that it is their lesson, and on the other hand, I feel guilty for not doing much, if anything, to help them. What is your advice?

The greatest disservice you can do to an impoverished individual is to feel sorry for that person and to see that one as weak. Each thought you have about an individual is received by that person. Honour your poor, for they are indeed as much God as you are. You can never know the real reason why individuals are in the position they are in. Stories abound of beggars and street peddlers living in expensive houses and driving expensive cars, and why? It helps you to justify why you are not helping them. And why do you entertain such stories? Because you are afraid that it may happen to you. Therefore, telling tales of poor people not really being poor enables you to mask your fear of poverty. But it is more fundamental than that, for you are not helping them if you too feel impoverished. Poverty exists because you allow it; it is part of your consciousness, and it stems from fear. Fear is the root cause of all of humanity's problems.

We are not saying that you are greedy, selfish, or even responsible for the poverty of another, but do not delude yourself. All things that occur in your world, in your belief system, are expressions of the collective consciousness. You allow poverty because you have beliefs concerning wealth and worthiness. You believe that you must work hard for all that you have in order to deserve it. When a person achieves wealth, a great celebration is made of how hard he or she has worked for it. In essence, wealth is the inheritance of each and every one of you, and it cannot be worked hard for; it is there for the receiving.

The greatest service that you can do for the poor is to give generously. Clearly, you cannot give to all, for your beliefs limit your ability to do that. As you pass beggars on the street, ask the Universe to connect you to the one that will make the best use of your help. We do not mean the best use in terms of what they do with your money, for that is their business, but we mean the best use in terms of their inward response to your gift. If you were to walk up to a street beggar and hand that person sufficient money to live on for several days, rather than a couple of coins of little worth, that has the effect of letting that one know that the Universe is indeed a hospitable and friendly place. This very action can assist the person to shift his or her beliefs about abundance and worthiness. This act of kindness on your part also works for you. It affirms your belief in unlimited resources and your ability to attract more wealth. It is a win/win situation. In that moment of grace, as you pass on your worthwhile gift, both you and the beneficiary vibrate with one another and harmony is created. As you give the gift, you affirm the other's ability to attract abundance, and you are likewise affirming your own ability. It is like a ballet of pure positive energy, lifting you both higher to a new level of vibration and harmony with the essence of abundance. As you assist others to grow, you yourself grow, for all energy that you put out into the world comes back to you!

Just as this book is inspiring you to be more than you are today, we encourage you to pass on these messages of truth. For as you are assisted by those just a step or two ahead of you, you too can assist those who are just a step or two behind you. For as you help another to grow, you in turn grow and prosper.

You have stated many times that feelings determine what we have and what we create. What are the best feelings for us to have when it comes to attracting money and abundance?

Two feelings are fundamental to the attracting of anything in your life: one is gratitude, the other is self-appreciation. When you look at your life with gratitude, you shift your focus onto what you like. As you shift your focus onto something, more of the same comes to you. That is the Law of Attraction. Gratitude does not work because the Universe says, "Look, there is one who is grateful, let us give this one more for they deserve a greater reward." The Universe is a neutral place and responds simply to your focus of attention. Gratitude places your focus upon the positive side of any subject; it places your attention onto the having of something, rather than the lack of something. As you practice gratitude and acknowledge what you already have, you shift not only your focus, but also your vibration, into the direction of *more* of the thing you are looking for. You see, *you cannot ask for anything that you don't already have.*

If you were born on an island somewhere where there were no birds and therefore no eggs, you could not ask for more eggs. It is the same with everything your heart desires. When you ask for abundance, you already have it. When you ask for health, you already have it. You see, if your legs lack health and you cannot walk, your arms still work don't they? Are you then totally devoid of health? No. Inwardly you *know* what health is because it is part of who you are. The Four Principles of Creation are who you are, they are not things you need to earn or discover. Perhaps you need to remember, but that is all, that is all. Health and well-being, abundance, love and the power to create are what you are. They are your very being, they are your soul, and they are the expression of the God/Goddess within you. We say to you with absolute knowing: You cannot ask for anything that you don't already have.

With gratitude you can focus on what is already present. For example, let us say that you are looking for an intimate relationship, one that provides you with companionship, love, sharing, and all the things you want from a partner. These things are already in your life, expressed by the people who are now in your life. Your friends offer you companionship, love, understanding, and many other things. When longing for a partner, most of you focus on your loneliness, and as you focus on the loneliness, you distance the opportunities for connecting with that special someone. When you acknowledge that what you want is already there and shift your focus onto it, you strengthen its presence and cause it to grow.

If you are one that says, "I cannot feel gratitude for I am so unhappy with my life," then let us say to you: Feelings are the result of thought; thought is the catalyst for all that you think. You can teach yourself how to feel gratitude by practicing it. Just as we have shared with you that you can deliberately practice self-appreciation in order to engender self-love, you can also practice gratitude and encourage that feeling within you.

When you want something to come into your life, sit and think of all aspects of it. Consider the essence of what it is that you want. If it is more money that you want, what does money represent to you? For many, money is synonymous with freedom. What else does it represent? Your ability to create an environment that is pleasing to you or any other thing with which you associate having money. Once you know what money represents to you and understand the essence of it in your life, begin to write down all the areas of your life in which that same essence is present. As you acknowledge where this essence already exists, you begin to attract more of the same. At the end of each day, write down all the things you are grateful for, all those things that contain the essence of the thing you want more of, and you will have gone a long way in shifting your focus onto the positive side of the subject of your desire.

Here are more examples to help you on your way. Let us say that money represents your freedom to travel and to explore. If this is the essence of what you want money to do for you, then you more than likely have that essence in your life already in the form of a car. Bless this car! All things have consciousness, awareness, even so-called inanimate objects such as cars, houses, and washing machines. Imagine that you are tuning into the essence of your vehicle and thank it for representing the essence of freedom in your life. You may want to thank your car each time you go on a journey and reaffirm that this vehicle is a manifestation of your desire for mobility and freedom. Your life is never void of what you want. It may be in a different form, or in a quantity that is short of where you want to be, but it is always there. We have observed that most of you who dwell in this place of wanting something, tend to focus on its lack. You lament your inability to travel, and see a world that keeps it far, far away from you. Through simple acts of gratitude you begin to shift your focus onto the having side of the equation.

Gratitude is not a spiritual obligation; it is not a spiritual law that 'good' and 'loving' people are expected to follow. It is the acknowledgement of the love already present in your life. It is using the Universal Laws to your benefit. As you acknowledge all things with gratitude, you begin to radiate love, and as you do this, you become magnetic to love, health and well-being, abundance, and the evidence that you are creator.

As we have stated many times, self-appreciation is paramount. There is nothing more important than that you feel good about who and what you are. As you acknowledge yourself with appreciation, you open the door to allowing more good things to come into your life. It no longer becomes a question of deserving or ability; it becomes a question of allowing. How much will you allow yourself to have today?

If there were nine thousand nine hundred and ninety-nine subjects upon which we could speak, and if you were to ask us which out of all these subjects was the most important, we would say to you, with an absolute knowing, without a shadow of doubt or the twinkling of a second thought, that self-appreciation is the most important topic of all. Self-appreciation is the key to your spiritual growth, to enlightenment, to humanity's problems; it is the solution to everything that is considered a problem.

For many generations you have been taught that to appreciate oneself is to be haughty and arrogant and unfitting. You have been told to keep yourselves small and not to think too highly of yourselves, for you are unworthy of such adoration and recognition. We bring you a different message. We say that it is time for you to appreciate yourself and that, without self-appreciation, all other things that you are striving for will either elude you or remain a struggle.

As you learn to appreciate who you are and what you have to offer the world, all the qualities that you want to develop, such as patience, acceptance, love, compassion, caring, and strength, will be yours. As is true in everything, that which is within you is reflected outside of you. That which you feel manifests in your world. Therefore, if you want to develop love, patience, and compassion, it is love of self, patience with self, and compassion for self that first must be developed. "You can only give what you already have." Does it not make complete sense to you when we say that? If you have but little love for yourself, then you will not be in a position to offer authentic love, i.e., acceptance, to another. You will offer a kind of ingratiation perhaps, telling yourself that you are loving and kind, but when you give love, there must be a two-way flow. The flow must come from an open heart, a heart that is also open to the receiver.

Many of you who focus on giving find it difficult to receive. Then, it is like using up the energy in a battery. The more you give, the more of your own energy you are giving away. When you are open to receive, then you become a conduit for the Universe, a channel for love. Pure Universal Love, the love of God, begins to flow through you. This love, this energy, is the source of all life, and as you become this channel, it feeds you, sustains you, keeps you in health and well-being, and allows abundance to flow freely into your life.

Self-appreciation is about saying: I accept myself exactly as I am. It is also about acknowledging your unique gifts. Your world is full of artists, healers, writers, great chefs, architects, teachers, and miracle makers who are yet to be discovered. They have not yet been discovered because you have not allowed yourself to shine. Within each of you is a highly creative, highly skilled being, just waiting to be discovered. Many of you catch glimpses of this in moments of inspiration, but then most of you immediately begin to compare yourself to others and tell yourself that their work or creation is of much more value than yours.

Self-appreciation is not about putting another down, or thinking you are better than another. It is about acknowledging the greater part of you, the part of yourself that is tapped into Universal knowledge and power and can create miracles. It is about acknowledging the truth of who you are. The truth of who you are is simple. You are a child of the divine, more than that even, you are the divine.

Somewhere along the line, many of you got the idea that you were here to prove yourself worthy of God or some other higher authority. This is not the case. You are here through the expression of your free will and you came forth into this plane of existence in order to create.

The Earth poses some unique challenges. It appears that there is much evidence suggesting that you are alone and not connected to the power of the Universe. But this is exactly why you chose to come here. It was a challenge that you were delighted to take. You are not here on probation; you will not be released from this place for good behaviour. You are not here waiting for the chance to go somewhere better. When your heart is filled with self-appreciation, it will govern what you draw to you. It will govern your experience of the world and how you relate to others. Then when you are fully self-appreciative, you will have the most delicious experience in the Universe. You will be physically focused, your heart will be fully open to the love of the Universe, and God's love will stream through you, using you as a channel for all that is great. There is no greater experience than this one, to be physical and spiritual simultaneously. This is why your planet is so populated, for many, many souls are wanting this experience, and self-appreciation is the key.

When you look at the great teachers, how do you think they got to that position? How did the Buddha and the Christ get to that position? It was through self-appreciation. It is only through loving and accepting yourself that you open yourself to the love of God. For God can only give you that which you are prepared to give unto yourself. There is no higher truth than that.

What are some of the main blockages to creating financial wealth?

All things in your physical world are representative of the non-physical; it is not any other way. Just as, when wanting to attract more of it into your life, we have encouraged you to find the essence of what you want, so it is your perception of the essence of money that will either repel it or attract more of it into your life.

Money is in a triangle of association with power and love. If you associate money with power and see power as dangerous, as something you are not to be trusted with, or as something that is harmful or lacking in love, then money will find it difficult to bless your life with its presence. Perhaps as a child you felt that you were offered gifts instead of the love and attention you wanted, or perhaps you resented those who seemed to have more money. There are many powerful beliefs in your society that have embedded themselves deep within your consciousness. You have sayings such as "filthy rich", "money doesn't grow on trees", "money is the root of all evil", and many others. Often people are hush-hush about money, sometimes feeling ashamed if they have too much or too little. In

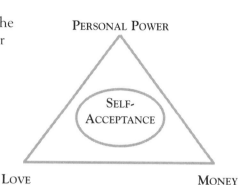

When there is a lack of money in your life, there is always a lack of self-love and feelings of powerlessness. Often, money is used to buy love or power, or inauthentic love (ingratiation) is used as a means to gain money or power. At the heart of this triangle is self-acceptance and self-appreciation. When you are in a state of self-appreciation, the triangle will be in balance.

many organisations salaries are kept secret for fear that those who have less will resent those who have more. Money is very powerful, and why? It is your physical manifestation of the energies of love and power.

When you have issues with money, you always, always, have issues surrounding self-love and appreciation and feelings of powerlessness. You either fear that you don't have any power, or that, if you do, it cannot be trusted. Money is not the issue, and never was. The issue is always about your perception of yourself and how you feel about who you are.

So many older souls struggle with money. Older souls often have a sense that they do not belong, or they wrestle with feelings of not wanting to be present on the planet. Often these older souls will be estranged from their families or will feel as if they are the 'black sheep', not fitting in with the rest of the biological family. This occurs because many older souls are born into families where the majority of members are of a younger soul age than themselves, and so have a different focus and view of life. This scenario is chosen because in their final lifetimes old souls choose the path of acceptance. If one who feels separated from family, there is often little or no real connection to the planet, no foundation or grounding. It is difficult for these souls to manifest in the material world for they are not fully present. To become enlightened involves being *fully* present on the Earth plane whilst being *fully* aware of the non-physical, balancing both worlds *equally* and accepting both. Part of this path means honouring the parents who have provided you with your blueprint for learning in this lifetime, for they made themselves available to you.

If it is what we feel which is most important in terms of creating abundance, why is it that some people have a lot of money although they are considered 'criminals', or unkind?

The experience of opposites can create strong desire. 'Criminals', as you to refer to them, are coming from a position of lack, for they must take or be involved in affairs in ways that are not for the greater good of all concerned. That sense of lack can engender in some an overwhelming desire for power. If money is then associated with that power, they will transfer much of their desire for power to money, thereby creating it in large quantities. When we speak of money, we speak in terms of generating abundance. A vast amount of money does not mean that you have abundance. Those who amass great sums of money in the pursuit of power always lack the ingredient of love in their life. As a result, they live fearful and often lonely lives, never able to form deep and lasting relationships. Yes, thought is powerful. If you want something enough, you can create truckloads of it. What we have suggested above are permanent ways to create lasting abundance. The 'criminal' may possess large financial resources until the end of this physical life, but will he or she have mastered love, acceptance, or allowing in their lifetime? No.

All the teachers who have told you that a focus on money will bring it to you are indeed correct. What we add to that is the emotional element that will assist you to create lasting abundance. For a full wallet and an empty heart are not abundance; they are still poverty.

Chapter 6

Prayer

What is the purpose of prayer? Does it help? Should we pray? If so, how should we pray?

When you pray, you are summoning forth the creative forces of the Universe. We have observed that when you pray, the vast majority of you pray from a position of lack. There are those of you who approach prayer as if you are beseeching the will of that which is greater than you. If you can appeal convincingly to that greater, more powerful being, then you will get what you want. We have said repeatedly that there is no higher authority in your life than you. Your will is dominant in the physical world. Within you is the power to create, within you is the wisdom of ages. They are not outside of you. When you pray from a position of lack, the Universe can only deliver to you more of the same. If you approach prayer from a position of feeling weak or incapable, then that image of yourself becomes dominant in your manifesting. However, this does not mean that you cannot call upon assistance, for there are many beings who are in service to humanity. What we encourage you to do is to acknowledge that you are able, and have the right, to summon forth energies unto yourself in a multitude of forms.

It is important for you to acknowledge that you are a multidimensional being. As such, the greater part of yourself is at one with the power that creates worlds, with what you call God. As you pray, you are literally summoning forth this power to create in your world.

This is a prayer we suggest: "Source of all life that is non-physical, may I always honour this part of myself. May your presence be expressed through me as it is expressed in other realms. Supply me with all my needs for today and release me from my limitations as I release others from their limitations. Keep me from illusion and deliver me from fear."

All words have energy, just as thoughts do. Words are thoughts expressed and they carry with them the message of your intention. Words are charged either with positive energies of love that help you to expand, or they are charged with the energies of fear that cause you to shrink away from who you truly are.

Try out an experiment now. Chant each of the following words for 30–60 seconds. After 15–20 seconds, you will have begun to resonate with the energy of a particular word, and as you begin to chant beyond the first 15–20 seconds, you will be bringing that vibration deeper into you, becoming the quality that the word expresses. First, chant the word "Joy". Notice what happens. How did you feel? Did you start laughing? Did a smile start walking across your face as if it had a mind of its own? Now try the opposite. Chant the word "Fear". What happened? What did your body do? Did you cross your legs? Start breathing in a different way? In this exercise, you started to resonate with fear, and your body began to react to that energy. Now chant the word "Love", and allow yourself to chant this word for at least a minute so that you can undo the energy of fear that was brought in as part of our experiment together.

Words have power. They summon forth compatible energies. So the words you speak have an impact on the way you experience your reality. If you constantly tell people how hard you are trying to find a new job, you will continue to create more trying hard. If you continue to tell people how you hate something, you will increase the amount of things that you hate in your life. Just as you have control over choosing what you think, you also have the power to consciously choose your words. No matter how you are feeling, you can change your mood and feelings simply by repeating an empowering word in your mind, or out loud, for a minute or two.

This may not change your mood for the rest of the day, but it will have lifted your energy temporarily, and every time you lift your energy, the more accustomed you will become to a higher vibration. And it will then become habit forming. Love and joy will become a habit, and that is a habit you probably will not want to break! Try these things out. I would rather you believe these things through experience than simply take my word for them. The next time you are in a place you do not particularly enjoy or your mood has taken a downward turn, spend some time repeating a word that gives you power and observe what happens. Words that carry positive energy are: Love, joy, abundance, trust, happiness, delight, laughter, yes, forgiveness, and any other words that energise you.

In addition to creative words, there are affirmations, statements that affirm how you wish to recreate yourself. Affirmations help you focus on a particular goal or desire. Affirmations are statements like: I am joyful and abundant; Abundance is my natural state of being; All good things come to me easily. It is important that all your affirmations are stated in the present tense.

Remember, the Universe always gives you exactly what you want, so if you affirm: I want a new home (with the feeling that you dislike where you are), then you will continue in your wanting of a new home. The Universe will agree with you: "Yes, you are *wanting* a new home." This may seem like a cosmic joke, but so many of you hold a vision of things in the future, that they continue to remain there—in the future! When you desire something and your desire for it is dominated by your dislike of what you have, the Universe cannot deliver it to you for you are focused on not having it. You can say, "I want a new home", and if you do so with the feeling of expectation and excitement, it will be yours.

Create your own affirmations and choose words that are the most empowering for you. Make the affirmations easy-to-remember ones that roll off your tongue effortlessly. An affirmation that is too long or complicated will not assist you to hold the mental focus on what you want. Once you have your affirmation, you can either dedicate a time of day in which you will chant your affirmation for 10 minutes or more, or you can repeat it to yourself as you go through the day. A combination of both is more powerful, and combined with visualisation you will be well on your way to creating whatever you desire.

For visualisations and affirmations to be powerful they have to be non-specific, not being attached to a particular object. If you are affirming that you want to find your soul mate, for example, you will be doing yourself and the other person a disservice by affirming that you want a particular person. Before starting, ask that what you visualise serves the highest good of all. Never bring into your visualisations a sense of competition with others, nor an intention that others meet with misfortune. What you send out comes back to you—that is a Universal Law and the Law of Attraction.

What is our greatest blockage to creating what we want?

The reason why most of you are not getting the things you want is because of the balance of your thinking. The vast majority of you pay much more attention to the lack of what you want than to focusing only on the having of it. In addition to this, you tend to set up resistance and other thought patterns that lead to the obstruction and undermining of your creations.

It is by getting into a downward spiral of negative thinking that you set up resistance to creating what you want. Many of you do this for a few minutes each day, and most of the time you are not even aware that you are doing it. Let us give you an example. You go to the grocery store and you want to buy some apples. On picking up a bag of apples you notice that a couple of the apples are rotten. Your thought continues:

Hmmm, typical. You'd think they'd put out good produce for the prices they charge.
Well, service and quality are not what they used to be.
It is always so difficult to get what I want.
It is the government's fault.
If it weren't for them, I could have what I want.

The Law of Attraction acts with thoughts as well as words and as you think the first negative thought, and couple it with an emotion such as frustration, anger or annoyance, you intensify the thought, which draws to itself a thought similar to itself. The next thought arrives, and so on and so forth, until you have a downward spiral of thoughts that have taken you far from your original intention.

Let us work with another example. You are walking through a shopping centre with the intention of buying new clothes for yourself, and you bump into a friend or colleague.

"Hi, how are you?"
"Doing fine, and you?"
"Just great! Wish it would cool off again, this weather is just too hot for me and the kids."
"I know what you mean. Mind you, I don't like it being cold either."
"Well, if you listen to the farmers, the weather is never perfect."
"I guess that means the price of bread will go up again."
"Well, isn't everything just getting more and more expensive?"
"I know, I can hardly make ends meet. Each month seems to be a bigger struggle than the month before."
"You know, they were laying off people at the supermarket last week."
"I know. I heard. My biggest fear is losing my job."
"Yeah, all this hard work and toil, makes you wonder what life is all about."
"Tell me about it. All I seem to do is work, work, work and have nothing to show for it."
"Well, I have to be off. Have a nice day!"
"Yes, you, too. Bye for now!"

Did you notice the downward spiral? Once you have offered that the energy of a conversation take a particular direction, and there has been a response to that direction, there must be a conscious choice to turn the energy around so that it may ride the upward spiral instead of the downward one. Although you may see such seemingly idle chat as harmless, we want you to understand that no chat is ever idle! No thought is ever idle! All thought is active and all thought creates. As you think these thoughts and confirm them with your words they proceed to go out into the Universe to bring you more of what you have offered in thought and word.

The real issue here is that most of you have become reactive beings instead of the conscious creators of your world and of your experience. What we mean by reactive is that you spend more time responding to circumstances than you do to giving thought to the circumstances you want to create. At the heart of all resistance is the belief that you are subject to the circumstances of the outer world. You believe that the actions of others, of governments and other authorities, control your life to such an extent that it is not possible for you to have what you want. Resistance has become such a large part of your society that nations have created armies and weapons of mass destruction in order to protect themselves against those things that they wish to resist. With your very resistance you are drawing to you that which you are resisting. Nothing outside you can exert itself upon you or influence you in any way whatsoever without your invitation. And the way you invite things into your experience is through giving your attention to them. You have heard the expression, "What you resist persists." This is a high truth indeed and these simple words express a deep understanding of the Laws of the Universe!

As a species, you have become so convinced that you need to resist that which you don't want to experience that you have created entire industries to keep things at bay. A pharmaceutical industry, defence industry, and charities that wage war against cancer, hunger, aids, poverty, ignorance, and all manner of things. You band together to form political groups, parties and forums that have the sole purpose of being against something that a particular group or nation doesn't want. Have any of these things changed? Have they become less, or is their incidence increasing? We hear you say, "But don't we have to face reality? These things do exist; they threaten us and exert themselves against us." And we say to you: Reality is the last thing you need to face! Whose reality? Theirs? Yours? It is your function to create the reality that you want to see and experience. This does not mean that each time you pass a beggar on the street you shrug your shoulders and say to yourself, "Well, that is his reality and I have nothing to do with it." What we are suggesting is that, if you feel drawn to help such individuals, you assist them from a position of prosperity and not from a position of lack.

If you were to assist this 'poor' man because you see him as being poor and in need of your charity, you are assisting him to remain exactly where he is, and adding to your own sense of lack at the same time. If you choose to assist this man with the attitude that you are, through your actions and words, simply reminding him of his natural state, which is that of abundance, you will go a long way to assist him in changing his reality into one that is more pleasing to him, if indeed that is what he wants.

As with our discussion on *karma*, it is not what you do that is important. The real key always lies in the thought and motive behind the action. It is the thought and motive that determine the energy that is shared with the ones you are assisting. Even without your words, they are aware on some level of the thoughts and energy behind your actions.

Chapter 7

Race

_____

Why are there so many races and what is the purpose behind having a multi-racial world?

To answer this question fully, it is necessary for us to go into the untold history of your world. The races on your world developed on different planets, not on the Earth as you know it today. This may seem bizarre or even heretical to you, but it is the truth as we know it.

Back in the mists of time, the Earth was colonised by many beings who originated from planets that exist beyond your solar system, planets that were part of other star systems in another part of the galaxy. "Primitive man" coexisted with these races, and there was some interbreeding, the introduction of new genes, and of a new evolutionary direction for the human species. Your scientists have quite accurately catalogued and recorded the evolution and development of your planet and of your species, but they are missing some vital information. Prehistoric races of humanity, such as Neanderthal man, evolved, developed, and died out quite naturally.

No colonisation of this planet took place until it could be clearly determined that the evolution of the humanoid species already here would not develop in such a way that would successfully support 'ensoulment'. Essentially, the species that were present were created by souls who wished to experience being 'semi-animal'. This experience is, and was, just as valid as any other. Each planet has a governing body. This governing body is a council that oversees the evolution of species and shepherds all life on and within a planet. In addition to this, there is a consciousness, a soul, which inhabits the planet itself, for just as you have a soul, or are a soul inhabiting a human body, the Earth itself has a soul that inhabits it. Therefore, all colonisation, or introduction of new species, cannot and does not happen unless the consciousness or guardians of that particular planet are agreed. So why did these new species come to Earth?

Throughout your galaxy, each planet has tended towards single race development. This is the equivalent of having a planet where only Swedish people live, or where only Japanese people or Europeans live. In that sense, there is not as much variety in terms of the cultural expression and language, although it does exist.

In terms of reincarnation and numbers of lifetimes, the majority of you have had hundreds, if not thousands, of lifetimes. Each sojourn upon a particular planet or world is called a cycle, and you may have as many as 200 to 300 lifetimes in one cycle. In the distant past, those of you who are on Earth today have had lives, indeed many lives, on planets that exist in other stellar systems within your galaxy. You have had many lifetimes in these other systems and have gained much experience living in cultures that were not as diverse as the one you exist in today. Having completed a cycle in these worlds, having reached enlightenment, you then sought new experience. Not only you, but many others like you, collectively decided that it would be a new experience for many different soul nations to come together in one place and develop together. This was a new and exciting challenge and it brought with it the lesson of acceptance of diversification.

> *"Having reached enlightenment,*
> *you then sought new experience."*

The souls who inhabited the bodies of primitive man no longer wished to continue with this experience as they had already gained all the experience they wanted at that time. New races developed through the introduction of new DNA from the 'visiting' races. These visiting races were humanoid and looked very much as you do now, with minor differences. Not all of humanity as it is today is the result of this interbreeding, for there were many humanoids that chose to stay. However, over the course of hundreds of thousands of years, there is more uniformity, although you clearly have the expression of different races.

The 'original' Earth races died out, but their genes live on in you, as do the genes of your forefathers who came from the stars. In a sense, we are talking here to two of you, the you who is your body, and the you who is your soul. The you who is your soul is the eternal part of you, and you are the same forefather of the species that is now the human body that you inhabit. In effect, it was your DNA in the physical body you inhabited then that has led to the creation of the body you experience now, because you have determined your own evolution. You are the creator and mastermind behind it. Some of you are indeed the very same beings that ensouled the bodies of 'primitive' beings that died out. None of this just happened, or just happened to you. It is by grand design.

Many of you have deeply buried memories of your connections to the stars. Some are faint memories of past lives in other star systems, and other memories come from recollections of the time when the creation of the races took place here on Earth.

So how did we get here, and where did we come from?

Highly advanced cultures carried out the seeding of the planet with new races. These were cultures that had mastered the power of thought and had incorporated 'thought power' into their technology. With this union of mind and machine, they were able to cross vast distances of space, for it was a case, literally, of mind over matter. There is one thing that does travel faster than the speed of light, and that is thought. Thought travels in an instant. The technology they developed was able to tap into and interpret the mental field of energy, i.e., the intention of the traveller. Therefore, 'distance' and 'time' became conditions that were no longer relevant to travel. It was as if they brought the destination to themselves, instead of 'travelling' to the destination.

As there was mass transport, and these beings were highly evolved, able to focus their thoughts on a specific objective for long periods of time, they were and are still able to travel great distances in a matter of minutes, often 'instantaneously'. These cultures understood consciously that time, space, and thought were not the separate things that many of you suppose. They understood the fundamentals of the Universe in terms of knowing absolutely that thought creates reality and that thought does this by moulding Universal energy into a form reflective of the creative thought. In this sense, the Earth came to them; they did not travel to it, for it was a manifestation of their collective desire and focused thought.

Essentially, many beings arrived in crafts, and those that were even more evolved simply materialised on the face of the planet. Have you not heard many stories of how spiritual masters have appeared to others in a different form? It is the same process. Once you have moved beyond fear, you understand that "I and the Father are one," meaning "I and the source of all creation are one." With this knowledge you are not only understanding fully and consciously that you are the creator of your own reality, but you are living that knowledge and are freely able to create and recreate, even creating a physical body!

Your body is energy that has coalesced into form. At the atomic level, there is space between the atoms, and these atoms are made up of even smaller parts, and so on and so on, until you reach a form of pure energy. This pure energy is manipulated and moulded by thought, and just as your soul has manipulated this very same energy to create the body in which you exist at this moment in time and space, these beings, some of which were you in another 'lifetime', were able to do this consciously. They were able to do this because they were aware of the superconscious mind and existed within that state of being. They experienced themselves as not only being the personality self which they were in the process of creating for the Earth experience, but were also aware of their multidimensional soul-self that has many aspects and transcends time and space. This 'past' is also humanity's 'future'.

Many of your ancient texts contain references to these events, although they are shrouded in superstition and written from the perspective of the writer at that time. The existing references to 'angels' having mated with human women (see Genesis 6:2) are referring to the time when indeed many beings came to Earth to partake in one of the greatest experiments ever created. These non-physical beings that were able to take physical form were very adept at manipulating matter, for they understood that all matter was coalesced energy that was moulded by thought. It was their ability to focus thought that has led to the recording of stories about individuals and groups that lived for 500 years or more. These beings understood that the body responds to thought and that bodily conditions that reflected lack of health, ageing, and death were merely manifestations of limited thinking. As interbreeding with 'primitive' man took place, and as the incoming population produced offspring through the same biological process to which you are accustomed today, the personalities became increasingly associated with physical form. With this association, which was all part of the plan, humanity began to focus on the physical dimension, which led to the 'forgetting' of their non-physical heritage, a heritage that spans hundreds of thousands of years across a vast galaxy of star systems. These memories have now been relegated to the record of vague stories, myths, and tales of a bygone age.

Much of your contemporary 'new age' literature makes reference to star systems such as the Pleiades, Sirius, Orion, and other star systems. This is not in the least bit new. These star systems have been referred to in your ancient texts (see Job 38) and are also part of many oral traditions that are held by tribal peoples across your globe. Many of these cultures, when asked where their ancestors came from, will freely and gladly point to the stars. They will tell you stories of 'gods' who visited them, mated with their women, or who brought them here long, long ago. Far from being the myths of a tribe, they are the record of how you got here. Yes, indeed, many of you originated from the Pleiades, Sirius, Arcturus, and other systems. However, this does not mean that these star systems are your true home, for your true home is within you. You are not a being 'lost' on a foreign planet, for your physical body has evolved to become an Earth body, made up of genes that are in origin both Earth **and** 'alien'. This means that you are a unique being that is indigenous to the Earth.

"Your true home is within you."

There are many of you who are beginning to experience faint stirrings within that are telling you that you are from elsewhere, that your origin is in another place altogether. These faint memories have caused many of you to draw the conclusion that you are far away from 'home' or that you 'don't really belong here', or that you don't fit in because your origin is 'different'. Home, my beloved ones, is where the heart is. Where you have incarnated previously has no relationship to where home is. So many of you are reaching a level of development where you are increasingly and more easily able to tap into higher consciousness, into the superconscious mind. Within this superconscious mind that transcends time and space, you are able to experience the memories, however faint, of a time when you lived in much more harmony than now. These memories are a bleed-through from your previous cycles.

"Home, my beloved ones, is where the heart is."

Yes, you have had many lives, tens of lives, where your life has been far more abundant and harmonious than now. However, we encourage you to reject the conclusion that Earth is a bad place, or a place where things have gone wrong. It is a new experience that you have chosen. Having created such harmony in your being before, you have chosen to recreate the same harmony under circumstances that are different and unique. It really is as simple as that. Rather than looking longingly to the stars, understand that these memories are a longing to return to the one place that will bring you home, and that is to your heart, for that is where home is. You create your own reality, not some of it, not most of it, but all of it. As you return to your heart, as you return to love, you begin to create a reality that reflects that state of being. It is a state of being where you are in total and complete acceptance of what is, where you allow all others to be who they are, and allow all conditions to reside, without letting them draw you out of your centre. For you who know that you are the centre of your Universe, to be centred once more in the heart will create for you a life that will be more like home than the home you imagine you are longing for. What you long for, my beloveds, is love. This is your greatest yearning. It is your will and longing to love that drives you, that feeds you, that keeps you going.

"It is your will and longing to love
that drives you, that feeds you…"

There are many stories about dolphins and their origin. How do dolphins and whales fit into the whole scheme of things?

Let us first speak of the dolphins, for the dolphins are more akin to you in terms of their mental, emotional, and spiritual development. Dolphins are just like humans. They think, they feel, they desire, they experience emotions, they express humour, displeasure, in fact, the entire range of human emotions. They are, in essence, sentient beings just as you are a sentient being. There are many who believe that dolphins are 'superior' to humans, possessing extrasensory powers. Although this is true for some dolphins, as it is true for some human beings, it is not true of all dolphins. Dolphins take part in the same process of reincarnation as humans do. They begin life on Earth as baby souls, young souls, learning about their world and how to interact with it, and gradually, over many lifetimes, begin to develop other skills and add a spiritual perspective to their lives. It is the same for human beings.

The history of dolphins, like that of humans, has two branches. There are those species that evolved and developed in their own right on Earth, and those that came to the Earth from another planet. Many have associated dolphins with the star system Sirius. This star system has within it a planet that is composed almost entirely of water; we will refer to this world as Delphi. This planet, like your own, has hosted ensouled species for many eons. Many of you have had many incarnations on this world, and on others like it, for Delphi is not the only 'water world' in existence. Once a soul's experience is complete, it then goes on to choose another. It is quite valid and common for a soul to experience tens of lives as a dolphin and then to choose a new cycle of experience as a human, or as another sentient being.

The forms taken by sentient beings vary widely throughout the galaxy. The more that humans learn about and from the dolphins, the more you will realise that God was made in man's image and that the images and variety of forms that God can take are as numerous as the stars in the heavens.

Human communication with dolphins holds the key to a great forward leap in your present evolutionary cycle. This breakthrough will come within a 10 to 20-year period from the delivery of this material. Conscious communication with the dolphins will change the way in which you look at your world and your position in the Universe, and will answer once and for all that age-old question, "Are we the only ones?" Indeed, you are not the only ones. The Universe is teeming with intelligent life, both physical and non-physical. However, it is the discovery of intelligent physical life, for that is your current focus, which will have the greatest impact on your culture. Just as your governments are putting much energy into the search for extraterrestrial intelligence, the search for terrestrial intelligence is quietly forging ahead in many corners of your globe.

There are those who already have telepathic contact with this aquatic species. However, telepathic contact alone will be insufficient to influence the minds of millions, for telepathy is not provable in terms acceptable to the majority. What will come along is a technology that will assist you to record and decipher the vast range of tones produced by dolphins. You will discover that they have names, grammar, oral traditions, and viewpoints. It will surprise many of you to find that not all dolphins agree with one another, and that many will tell their own variations of a similar story.

The dolphins will help you understand your own development and clearly see that the levels of development that exist within humanity are also found amongst dolphins. In addition, they will communicate to you their own history. Their larger cousins, the whales, have recorded much of this history. From this history, you will learn much about your origins. The whales will assist humanity to fill in the gaps that modern-day science has not yet been able to explain. This breakthrough in communication will be the single most significant event to occur on your planet for many thousands of years. There have been other very significant events such as the incarnation of the Christ and of the Buddha; however, this event, the conscious communication with dolphins, will change in almost every way how the human species currently looks at itself, its position, and its relationship to other species. For example, the dolphins will give you an entirely new way to look at your relationship to the animal kingdom. Your classifications and grouping of animals will change overnight. You will begin to relate differently to horses, bovines, pigs, and domestic dogs and cats. This information will change your relationship to animals forever, and a great teacher will emerge to assist humanity to adjust to this new view. Then, and only then, will humanity be ready to be introduced to the larger, broader family. This 'family' is made up of the descendants of ancestors that originated from other star systems.

There has been much talk about UFO's and beings from other worlds. Although these beings exist and there has been contact with individuals, and sometimes with tribes, in recent millennia, large-scale contact with the human species is not expected to take place until after the contact with the dolphins and whales. Humanity is preparing for this contact and many of your films are introducing the idea that you are not alone. The issues that are played out in dramatic productions are an expression of your current consciousness.

Now that religion has largely lost its grip on humanity, and science has not been able to provide all the answers, many are expecting the answers to come from the stars. However, at this moment in time, any large-scale contact with extraterrestrial races would be more destructive than constructive. This is not because such races are malicious, rather they are benevolent, but it would be destructive because the majority of human beings are not in a position to integrate the psychological, philosophical, religious, and political changes that such contact would bring. Overnight, your search for who you are would be over, and your history would be rewritten in an instant. No established culture could survive such a dramatic change. This is where the dolphins will play a vital role for humanity.

Your contact with the dolphins will be step one in a transformation of your species that will eventually lead to your inclusion within the greater family of humanity. The 'space' films presented to you are a direct reflection of your collective curiosity and search for answers to age-old questions. These films also serve the purpose of opening you up even more to the possibility of contact with other sentient beings and helping you to prepare on an emotional and psychological level for the inevitable changes to come.

It is important to add that your species has not been intentionally excluded from the greater family of humanity. Your exclusion has been a reflection of your consciousness. You create your own reality, not only as individuals, but also collectively as nations, races, and as a species. Your collective consciousness focused itself towards Earth, towards physicality, and towards the experience of separation. This experience of separation has provided you with the comparison that you were looking for, for as you experience separation, you are in a better position to understand oneness.

The primary incentive for creating the Earth experience was to construct a civilisation that had as its goal the acceptance of diversification. This goal in itself caused all who are involved in this adventure to focus on their individuality to such an extent that you perceived yourselves to be alone. When beings perceive themselves to be alone, or cut off from source, alienated from God, they invariably create their own God and associate themselves strongly with that God. When this occurs, religion develops along with a cultural identity. All those who feel alone then begin to associate with other beings that seem similar to themselves, as a way to circumnavigate the feelings of separation. It is in this way that races, cultures, languages, religions, and political groups evolve.

Your ancestors experienced the same thing, but they did not become aware of other cultures until such times as their technology allowed them to travel beyond the confines of their planet and solar system. There were, and are, many advanced cultures that are quite singular in their expression. Although they are spiritually developed, their view of the Universe and the nature of God is very much based on their perception of themselves, from their own unique cultural perception. It is for this reason that various similar species agreed together at the very highest level to come to Earth in order to create the same evolution and the same growth with the inclusion of much diversity.

This acceptance of diversity is being played out in many regions of the world, in particular in areas where there are concentrations of mature and old souls, many of whom are the original souls that migrated to your planet for this very purpose. The areas we are speaking of are the European Union, the United States of America, Israel, and South Africa. Another example is Brazil; however, like Israel, it is working with issues surrounding religion. It is not that religion is not an issue in the other regions mentioned; there is simply a different focus.

Chapter 8

Reincarnation

You, like many other non-physical and physical teachers, speak of reincarnation. Why do we live so many lives?

First, let us tell you what reincarnation is not. Many of you think you reincarnate so that you may evolve. That is not its purpose, although, on one level, it is exactly that, a path of evolution. However, you did not go to Earth to improve yourself, or to become good enough to go elsewhere. Earth life is an experience. You were not sent as an imperfect soul to Earth so that you might become perfect through many lifetimes. Quite the contrary. You **chose** the Earth experience in order to increase your skill. You who read these words are already enlightened beings of light, 'Masters'. As a Master, you chose to add physicality to your distinctiveness and you did this because physicality presents unique challenges and is indeed one of the more 'challenging' schools. So far from being the 'dunces' of the Universe, you are skilled souls who chose a belief system (reality) that would greatly increase your skills.

You are a multidimensional being. As such, not only are you focused in physical reality, but there are parts of your being that are conscious and present in 'higher' dimensions of reality, even as you read this book. Can't you sense the energy that is close to you now, feeling as if it is reading along with you? That is your Greater Self; it checks in on you, always wishing, always waiting for you to become aware of it. This causes great celebration, for this is the greater purpose of your Greater Self, your Soul Self. The deepest desire of the soul is to become fully conscious whilst in the physical body. Some have called this enlightenment, others have called it ascension, and we call it becoming fully conscious.

> *"The deepest desire of the soul*
> *is to become fully conscious whilst in the physical body."*

When we refer to young soul, mature soul, old soul, etc., we are not talking about age. We are talking about experience. Although in the majority's experience, 'old' souls have had more lifetimes than 'young' or 'baby' souls, it is possible for a 'mature' soul to have lived many more lives than an 'old' soul.

So what do we mean when we speak of soul ages? We refer to experience, and this experience is about becoming increasingly aware of the total self whilst in the physical state. Those of you who are seekers of truth and of self are responding to the impulses of your Greater Self, your Inner Being, your Soul, for it desires that you should know it, and it desires to know itself through you. Your Inner Self desires to be fully conscious through you, while being at one with the All-That-Is. Soul age is determined by the individual soul's level of skill at being consciously present in the physical plane.

What is a Soul Mate?

There is much conjecture and misunderstanding concerning this subject. When most of you speak of a soul mate, you are thinking of that one special individual that you will fall in love with and with whom you will live happily ever after. You may even feel as if this one special love has always been your lover through many, many lifetimes and that you are simply awaiting his or her appearance in this lifetime.

Many souls do encounter one another in lifetime after lifetime after lifetime, for they have become friends. This friendship is based in the non-physical world, and the friendship, which in essence is co-operation, is based upon their past success in achieving the growth they are seeking. You see, you are growth-seeking beings, and all encounters, both physical and non-physical, provide opportunities for growth. Therefore, if there is a certain soul with whom you have had great success in achieving your goals, you are likely to agree to work with that one again.

> "You are growth-seeking beings, and all encounters, both
> physical and non-physical, provide opportunities for growth."

It is important to understand how souls are organised. Your journeys here into the physical world are deliberate journeys. You have already mastered life on many other planes of existence, and your purpose for coming to Earth is simply so that you may broaden your experience of yourself through the Earth existence. The ultimate goal is to experience unconditional love, that which is acceptance and allowing. For as you totally accept Earth life and accept all the aspects of it and all that exists within it, you have reached your goal. Some have called this enlightenment. You see, you didn't come here to get better or to prove yourself worthy; you came here for the fun of it, for the game, for the challenge.

*"The ultimate goal is to experience unconditional love,
that which is acceptance and allowing."*

Before such journeys are undertaken, souls organise themselves into groups. You could see these as support groups. Souls organise themselves into Families, Groups, Clans, Nations, and Grand Nations. There are seven souls in a Soul Family and seven families in a Soul Group, and seven groups in a Soul Clan, and so on. Eventually, you will work with most members of your Soul Clan, that is 343 individual souls. However, for those of you who are teachers, you will more than likely reach your Soul Nation or Grand Nation, which totals almost 17,000 souls.

The majority of your relationships, close friendships, and associations will be with souls who are from your Group of 49 souls. However, this is not always the case. The more you advance in terms of acceptance (love), the more skilled you will become at working with individuals who have a different energy signature than yourselves. What we mean by energy signature is the following: each Soul Group will be working towards a particular goal.

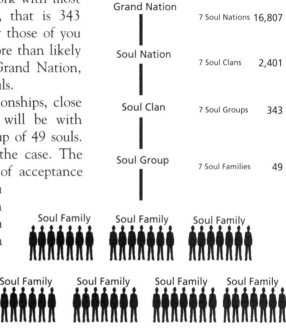

For example, many members of one Soul Group could be concerned with communication and teaching, another with healing, another with courage, another with self-acceptance. This does not mean that each of you will manifest in the same way and lead identical lives, but it does mean that the essence of your lives will be very similar. You will have similar ideals, aspirations, likes, and dislikes. The people you are most drawn too are almost always members of your Soul Family, Group, Clan or Nation, but as with everything, there are exceptions to the rule.

A Soul Family will work together for many, many lifetimes. Sometimes a Soul Family will regroup and different alliances will be made. This is rare, but it happens. In addition, the entire Soul Family will be involved in decision making regarding future lifetimes and will assist you in assessing your achievements in a lifetime just past. Your Soul Family is always there for you. For the most part, not all members of a Soul Family are incarnate at the same time. Those members who are not incarnate act as spirit guides during the physical life of the one who is incarnate. They can visit you in dreams, inspire you with thoughts, or in some cases, speak to you directly during meditation. Many of the spirit guides that have presented themselves to humans are indeed discarnate souls who are members of the individual's Soul Family. However, many of the Master Teachers that present themselves to humans are either members of the individual's Nation or Grand Nation and are souls whose Earth experience is complete. At times these Master Teachers can be souls that are even broader and vaster than this.

A soul mate is any soul that is a member of this broader group and anyone that touches your life. The net effect of a soul mate on your life will always be positive, even if you cannot see it at the time. For example, many have the notion that a soul mate relationship will be the ideal relationship, full of harmony and love. However, a relationship with a soul mate is likely to be challenging!

The whole point of a soul mate turning up in your life is to show you to yourself. That is the purpose of all human relationships. You learn through viewing in the mirror. The Law of Attraction works in every aspect of your life, and therefore each person drawn into your life is there through vibration, and nothing else. They are present because your vibration and their vibration are matched in some way. As we have said before, you are growth-seeking beings. So many of you get confused when you meet the person of your dreams, fall happily in love, declare, "This is my soul mate," and then have to pick up the pieces a few years down the road when the relationship breaks up or the person you loved turns out to have some problems or personality traits you do not care for. However, this was your soul mate, and you have many!

"You learn through viewing the mirror."

As you re-enter each lifetime, you make agreements with many different souls, perhaps as many as 20. You agree on what you will offer one another. These souls can be your children, your best friend, husband, wife, worst enemy, boss, business partner, any number of possibilities, and even the schoolteacher that encouraged you with patience and kindness. However, as you, the personality, have free will, you may create a path that takes you in a different direction, and this is why you have to make possible agreements with so many. The Universe works on the principle of vibration.

Let us give you an example: There is Joe who is a fine soul indeed. However Joe, for quite a few lifetimes now, has been struggling with powerlessness in the physical realm. His struggle has led him into violence and even to developing addictions to alcohol. Mary, on the other hand, for some time now has had difficulties in valuing herself, always choosing second best, and always giving her power away. So Joe and Mary coordinate their lives and set up a strong probability to meet. Their intention is that Mary and Joe will fall in love and work towards resolving their respective issues. In her relationship with the alcoholic Mary will learn that she must begin to make choices that reflect her self-worth. Joe, on the other hand, wants to learn that he cannot possess or control anyone, for power must come from within. However, Mary finds herself often challenged during the course of her life, and at college the establishment challenges her ideas and values. Instead of capitulating, as was her custom in previous lives, she stands up for herself and chooses to value herself. At that moment her vibration changes and therefore Joe is no longer necessary.

It could happen that she may meet Joe, but it would more than likely be a passing meeting and one in which she could share with him what she had learned. She may indeed end up being the counsellor at an alcohol rehabilitation centre, for example, but Mary no longer requires an intimate relationship with Joe. At this stage both Joe and Mary set up new vibrations so that they connect with their other possible soul mates.

When you look back at your life, you will see there are many people who have had an impact on it. All of these people are your soul mates, and whether they know it or not on the personality level, they love you dearly for you are all working together towards one singular goal, and that is the goal of love.

When we meet someone and an instant friendship or attraction occurs, does that mean that this is a soul mate and that we have been together in past lives?

What it means is that there is compatibility in vibration, and this generally means that there is a connection of sorts. Whether that soul be from your Soul Family, Group, Clan, or Nation, there is a connection, a similarity of goal, purpose, experience, and therefore vibration. However, this connection on the soul level does not automatically indicate that you have met before. You may never have met on the Earth plane, but the soul may be known to you in the non-physical world. You do spend rather more time in the non-physical than you do in the physical, for the non-physical world is your natural home. In the non-physical world you have friends in very much the same way that you have friends on Earth. Some friends are close to you, others are intimately acquainted with you, and still others are acquaintances. Friendship in the non-physical world has nothing to do with liking or not liking one another; it has to do with compatibility of goals and aspirations. Your non-physical friends also change, and they change according to your goals.

For example, you may have teamed up with a particular small group of souls to work on survival issues. Each of you have had a few lives together in inhospitable environments. You may have chosen to live in primitive cultures in very cold climates or in desert regions. Such inhospitable environments help you to become resourceful, inventive, creative, and self-sufficient. You may however, choose to return to this adventure at a later stage and not complete all of your 'learning' in one go. Or, you may progress at a faster pace than your group members and decide to move on. Another choice could be to remain with the group and become a leader or teacher amongst them, assisting them to progress, which in turn assists you to progress even further for there is much learning to be done whilst teaching. The possibilities are endless and the choice is yours. If you decide to move on, you will join another group, or perhaps work with one or two other souls. Your work with other souls may last one Earth day, an entire lifetime, or several hundred lifetimes. You choose all of these relationships, and each relationship is based on cooperation and the desire to progress as quickly as possible.

Are our parents and children Soul Mates and are they part of our Soul Family?

They are soul mates inasmuch as you not only know them, but you have chosen to work with them for the specific purpose of achieving growth. No birth is an accident, for all souls enter this world by agreement with both parents, even if both parents are not present in childhood.

Your parents and siblings may very well all be members of your Soul Family, but this is extremely rare. Normally, one, perhaps two, members of your biological family will be from your Soul Family, but the rest will generally be from your Group, Clan, Nation, or Grand Nation.

For the creation of a physical family the younger, less experienced souls will tend to team up with souls that are very closely related to them. These souls will often swap roles with one another from lifetime to lifetime, sometimes being the child, at other times the parent, at one time the female, at another time the male mate. The familiarity of the souls, one with another, helps each individual soul to progress more quickly. When souls first enter the physical plane, it seems to them to be a hostile place indeed. They are confused and wary of the physical body and are very susceptible to the biological impulse to survive. They are often caught up in fight or flight choices. The Universe is loving and supportive, and therefore it creates feelings of security to be surrounded by souls with whom you are very familiar. However, as with everything in the Universe, this is only general. It is not a hard and fast rule, for older souls can and do enter into these kinds of arrangements.

Many older souls choose to be born into families where perhaps only one member is well known to them, and perhaps this soul is from their Soul Group or Clan, not as closely related as a Soul Family member. They will make this choice because older souls are really concerned with introspection more than anything else. They may be preparing to teach or to become a leader in one field or another, and the experience of feeling 'the odd one out' will lead them towards self-examination. Instead of getting caught up with the function and duty of 'family' these souls will often be seen to be the 'black sheep' or viewed as different or eccentric by other members of the biological family.

Although these circumstances may lead to difficult personal challenges, the lessons are almost always internal rather than external. This means that there will be an emphasis on self-acceptance. Self-acceptance is an integral part of soul development. If we were to liken the Earth experience to education, mastering self-acceptance is equivalent to studying for your doctorate. Once you have self-acceptance under your belt, you are pretty much on the home run!

Why do so many of us search endlessly for the 'one true love' in the hope of finding our soul mate?

What you are looking for is acceptance. You believe that this 'one true love' will accept you without conditions. Your search for that one is in fact the search for self-acceptance. Each relationship is there to provide you with a new opportunity to know yourself. It is through knowing yourself that you can then grow to accept yourself and to love yourself. The one true love is self-love; there is no other love.

> "Each relationship is there to provide you with a new opportunity to know yourself."

The greatest secret of all, discovered by the Christ and the Buddha and many others, was the secret of falling in love with the self. When you love the self, you are in a state of acceptance, total acceptance. As you accept, you cease resisting the world and all that is in it. As you give up resistance, you allow everything to be as it is. As you allow everything to be as it is, God can work through you. It is at this point that you can say, "I and the Father are one," for you will be at one with the source of all life. You will be at one with love!

How many lives does a typical soul have on Earth?

A soul may have as little as one Earth life or as many as several hundred, or a thousand or more Earth lifetimes. Typically though, a soul will have 250-350 lifetime experiences, incarnating on an average of once per century. However, a soul may choose to skip a couple of centuries and then incarnate in rapid succession for several lifetimes in a row, perhaps only being discarnate for a year or two between lives. The average 'gap' is about 40 years, but that average has reduced considerably for many. This has occurred because humanity is at a major junction in its evolutionary progress and many souls want to participate in these exciting times.

The purpose of any soul entering the Earth plane is to master life on Earth. Souls that enter the physical realm are already experienced in other realms of existence. Contrary to a general concept that many hold, it is not 'unevolved' souls that enter into the physical world in order to prove themselves worthy of being elsewhere. The Universe is driven by thought, and thought is forever evolving and imagining new scenarios for itself. It is through this process that the physical world came into existence. In essence, the physical world became a new playground in which souls could experience themselves.

The Universe is built upon the principle of love and this principle pervades all other things. Love says that all is acceptable and that all is allowed. If there were no love, there could not be free will. Love and a lack of freedom cannot live together, for love is freedom. It is allowing. The essence of God is love and the Four Principles of Creation define the qualities of the divine. These qualities are love, health and well-being, abundance, and creativity. Each soul understands that it is defined by these divine qualities and experiences its true nature through these qualities. In striving for new experience, a soul always seeks to experience the embodiment of the four principles and therefore experience the divine essence within. The purpose of a soul entering the Earth plane is to fully experience the four principles of creation whilst in physical form.

> "If there were no love, there could not be free will. Love and a lack of freedom cannot live together, for love is freedom, it is allowing."

In essence, what we are saying is: Life is intended to be a joyous, delicious experience. The meaning of life is to live it, and to live it fully!

When you understand that you are in the physical dimension by choice and that you are not here to prove yourself worthy, you begin to realise that you are indeed creator. As a creator you came forth into the physical world to create experience. Part of this creative experience has been the encountering of comparisons or opposites. The experience of opposites has served you in your journey, for when you are in the midst of experiencing that which is not pleasurable, you are in the best possible position to begin stating, and therefore creating, that which brings you joy. Your challenge has been to realise that the physical world is an illusion and that your consciousness is not a result of physical biology, but that the biology and all that is physical is a result of consciousness, for the physical world is indeed your creation, your playground.

Opposites serve to awaken you to who you are. For the most part, conditions of suffering served you to reach higher, to reach within. As you descended into the physical dimension, you knew that you would forget who you are, that you are truly a non-physical being. The experience of pain and suffering has caused you to yearn for that which is higher, for that which is in alignment with the true nature of your being. Although pain and suffering are not your natural states, they have served you inasmuch that they have catapulted humanity forward into a clearer definition of where it wants to go. This is evident when we look at the two major wars that were created and experienced by your culture in the 20th century. These wars have propelled you forward and ushered in many fundamental changes. Today, you are much more concerned than ever before about freedom of choice, freedom from rules, and freedom for individuals to choose their lifestyles. This heralds the opportunity for the soul to become increasingly more present, for as the personality is freer to choose lifestyle, so the individual has more opportunity to experience essence. The more essence a personality experiences, the more it will be drawn to express essence. As this happens, the soul becomes increasingly the captain of the ship, and peace and harmony ensue.

It typically takes many lifetimes for a personality to reach the stage where it feels the influence of the soul. For those of you who are more mature and older souls, this will feel like a sense of mission. Your inner self draws you to achieve goals that feel as if you are being led. These goals usually are orientated towards service and some kind of creative expression. The drive can also be in business, but there will usually be an element of the kind of business that is about community service and motivating others to succeed. This entire process of evolving from survival to service typically takes 200 to 300 lives.

Once this level of personal evolution is achieved, the individual personality increasingly comes under the influence of the soul. Decisions that the personality makes are no longer based on logic but are driven by inner feelings, for the soul communicates to you through feelings and emotions. There was an agreement made prior to physical incarnation that the lines of communication between the soul and the physical personality self would at all times be open. Because you came to the planet with the intention of mastering Earth life through manifesting the four principles of creation in your life, the soul has the intention of guiding you and assisting you to achieve that goal.

The soul understands that each thought you have is creative, for it understands that it is creator and you are creator. As you think a thought, you launch a new creation. As you think the same thought often, you solidify the creation and it manifests in your physical reality. As you think a thought or entertain an idea that draws you away from the stated life goal, you soul will communicate to you with negative emotion. The purpose of the emotion is to steer you away from the thought that you are having. Likewise, when you are having thoughts that support the creation of your life goal, your soul will encourage you with positive emotion. Thought precedes emotion. So when you are experiencing emotion, it is always as a result of thought.

It generally takes several lifetimes for you to understand this process and to master it. It is only now that many of you are truly beginning to understand on an intellectual level that you do indeed create your own reality. With this realisation, many also understand the function of emotion and that, in order to fulfil your life purpose, joy and passion are the emotions that are to be followed. Many of you have for so long held to the belief that the path to God or to enlightenment is the path of suffering. Suffering has served you in teaching you all about who you are not and what you do not want. The new teacher is joy. It is not that joy is new, but that you are only now awakening to it, for your evolution has taken you to the stage where you can feel the true essence of your soul. This is truly a new dawn, this is the return of the Christ, this is the awakening of the God/Goddess within, this is the dawning of the new age. It is not an external event, but an inner event that is being led by the armies of joy!

"The new teacher is joy."

Most of you take an average of 200–350 lifetimes to reach the state of being fully blended with your Soul Self. However, there are souls who accomplish this task in a much shorter span of time, perhaps in 50 lifetimes or so. This is rare, but not unheard of. Those of you who are attracted to the material transmitted here are mature and older souls who are nearing completion of your journey in the physical plane.

What happens once we are complete with our journey of many lifetimes on Earth?

The possibilities are endless. You will initially spend time in what is the astral plane, perhaps as a Guide or a Minister. Ministers are beings who attend to the needs of those who are leaving the physical plane. They perhaps assist them to leave their physical bodies if there are difficulties and assist to create an atmosphere that is comforting for the new arrival in the non-physical realm. They are present around those who are in the process of dying physically and keep a focus of love upon them, transmitting day and night thoughts of peace, love, and harmony. Most of you choose to do this, at least for a short while, and many of you experience doing this, not only after your cycle has been completed on Earth, but also between lives and sometimes at night as you sleep.

Some of you then go on to become teachers. You sit on advisory boards that assist souls to make wise choices concerning their next incarnation, or you spend time communicating with incarnate souls whilst their bodies are asleep. You may even choose to study further and indeed teach at the Seven Schools of Enlightenment. These schools are present in the astral and higher planes of existence and serve as repositories of information and experience. Souls gather there to share in the experience of their forerunners and also to pass on their experience to those who will follow after them.

Chapter 9

Why do Some Souls Travel into Darkness?

Why do some souls travel far into darkness and others do not?

Everything you experience is an experience created within your own consciousness, whether you acknowledge that or not. The Law of Attraction, also known as the Law of Resonance, states that all things that are like unto themselves will be drawn. This law applies to everything, including thought. Energy in the Universe moves in spirals, and there are upward spirals as well as downward spirals. Your thoughts not only generate energy, but are in essence forms of energy in their own right. Thoughts gather thoughts; they magnetise to themselves thoughts of a similar nature. It is for the producer and observer of the thought to determine whether or not the thought being generated is pleasing. In this way, thoughts naturally evolve, and they can evolve in any direction. So you think a thought, let's say you are daydreaming about winning the lottery. One thought of wealth and joy attracts another, and you keep on adding more bounty, more abundance, more joy to the picture you have made of yourself winning the lottery.

The same is also true for thoughts that are on the downward spiral. As you imagine or talk about something that you perceive to be a negative happening, your natural inclination is to add another thought of a worsening situation to the thought you have just had, then another, then another until you imagine the worst case scenario. For many of you, this degeneration of thought is sufficient to stop you in your tracks and prompt you to once again move onto the upward spiral of thought.

The more conscious of its thoughts a being is, the more likely is this being to either remain on the upward spiral for the most part, or to halt the descent on the downward spiral once awareness of the situation has crept in. Because all thoughts are not only creative but also magnetic to that which is like them, many of you end up with many unwanted conditions. Your attention to a subject is sufficient to lead you onto either an upward or a downward evolutionary spiral.

Have you not noticed that those who speak of danger experience more of it? That those who speak of misfortune have more of it? That those who speak of wealth and opportunity also have more of that? Each of your thoughts is creative. You are **the creator**; you are the 'God' in your life. We can say this from an position of absolute knowing, for you are the physical extension of a vast multidimensional being that is not only a part of God, but is that which you conceive to be God at the highest levels. This means that you have **within** you the **same** creative force that created the planets and the galaxies, the same force that created your world.

> *"Have you not noticed that those who speak of wealth and opportunity also have more of that?"*

As a soul matures and gains experience, it begins to focus more clearly on that which fulfils it. In doing this, it lets go of rules and limitations and starts to see itself for who it truly is, a 'god' in human form. It is for this reason that great Masters such as the Nazarene and the Buddha were able to perform miracles, manipulate matter, walk on water, for they knew that not only could they manipulate all things and draw to them the subject of their attention, they also knew that they were one with this power, that the 'Father' and they were one.

The maturation of a soul usually takes many, many lifetimes, perhaps 200–300 on the physical plane, before it can manifest itself as a mature or older soul. However, this does not mean that only young souls experience negative conditions, or that mature and older souls only experience positive conditions. The 'age' of a soul is not determined by the amount of lifetimes it has had, but by its skill at being consciously present within the personality. However, as a general rule, mature and older souls have indeed had more lifetime experiences than infant and younger souls. This distinction of soul ages is not indicative of hierarchy, for all souls are equal. All souls are considered a Master at one level or another. On the Earth plane the difference between old and young souls is in how they manifest themselves.

As a soul progresses, it gains experience. Each lifetime is recorded within the overall consciousness of the soul. It can draw upon this experience and use this knowledge for future Earth life experiences. The more often a soul returns to physical experience, the more adept it becomes at making a conscious connection with the personality that it manifests. As this connection becomes clearer and clearer over many lifetimes, it brings the personality-self into alignment with the true nature of the soul. It is the true nature of the soul to always travel on the upward spiral. Therefore, there is a tendency for older souls to experience a more harmonious life, and a tendency for younger souls to experience less harmonious lives or even lives dominated by drama and trauma. We do not offer this information so that you can assume that all those you know who experience negative conditions must be less experienced or younger souls; we speak only of a tendency. All souls are capable of creating harmony and beauty just as all souls are capable of creating disharmony and chaos.

Conditions are created by thought. As you begin to observe your conditions and the thoughts that created the conditions, you will then become more skilled at using deliberate intention to think only of those things that are in alignment with harmony and joy.

"Conditions are created by thought."

So why do young children and babies experience negative conditions?

This question assumes that an infant is 'innocent' and unable to create with its thinking. This is far from the truth. Humanity has for a long time assumed that those that cannot talk, cannot think. This has moulded your relationships with the animal kingdom and with your children.

From the time a soul has formed the clear intention to come into the physical dimension, and it has been ascertained that the pregnancy will be carried full term resulting in a host body for the incoming soul, there exists telepathic contact between infant and both parents. It is this mechanism that contributes to the forming of the new emerging personality, for the telepathic link to both parents connects the child to its parents' thoughts and emotions. Essentially, the infant inherits a mixture of both the father's and mother's emotional makeup, in addition to elements brought with it based upon previous physical experience. In this way, a unique personality is created. The difference between one sibling and the next is determined by the experience of the incoming soul and also the prevailing emotional and mental condition of both parents at the time of conception through to birth and early childhood life. This applies even if one parent is not present, for example, if the mother dies after the birth of the child or if separation takes the father out of the presence of the child.

In the case of adoptive parents, links are still maintained with the biological parents, as well as new links formed with the adoptive parents. It is for this reason that many adopted children are compelled to search for their biological parents: their consciousness has been linked in such a way that the biological parents have played a key role in the creation of the personality, whether or not they have been physically present.

It is through these links that children will easily take on the thoughts and ideas of their parents. Fearful parents will generally raise fearful offspring. In your culture most parenting is based on warning young ones against the dangers of the world that they now find themselves in. As the child absorbs the beliefs and fears of the parents, it automatically begins to think in similar ways and develop similar fears. These thoughts and fears are as creative as any other thoughts, and the child then becomes the creator of its own reality, just as the parents are.

All souls choose their parents; there are no exceptions to this. A soul not only chooses its parents and its gender, but also chooses the country and culture where it wishes to be born, and what conditions prevail. The choice is made according to the experiences the soul wishes to have in a given lifetime. For example, a soul may set up conditions that are opposite to what it actually wants to achieve. This is a common choice. For example, a soul that wishes to experience great wealth may choose to be born into poverty, because this will assist it to thrust itself towards its goal. This is called comparison, and very often comparison helps you know what you want. In the case of a soul choosing poverty, to be born into what it does not want will spur it forward and make the personality hungry for wealth. This is a good motivator.

A soul may spend several lifetimes on this one project alone. It may make several attempts to achieve this. Perhaps in one lifetime financial wealth is achieved through crime and the exercise of domination, control, and manipulation. However, the soul will always seek to create the experience it wants through the exercise of love, for it is only through love that a state can become permanent. Once a soul has manifested wealth through the exercise of love, it then becomes a permanent aspect of its Earth-self and in all subsequent lifetimes the acquisition of money will be easy and comfortable for this being. However, once a soul has achieved this skill, it is not likely to continue as the focus. For example, a soul that has striven to create financial wealth over many lifetimes and finally succeeds in doing so out of love, may have a different focus after completing the experience. However, it will almost always find the creation of wealth to be easy. It will seem to have the 'golden touch' for this is now an aspect of this soul's identity.

"All souls choose their parents;
there are no exceptions to this."

This example also applies to fame. Your path to fame may have started with notoriety several lifetimes ago; perhaps as a person of great political or financial power who used fame only for personal gain. As you evolve over a period of many lifetimes, your focus will increasingly be on using fame and power for the benefit of humanity and your local community.

When a soul prepares itself for incarnation, it does not have a choice of all prospective parents on the planet; its choice is limited by its vibration.

Everything in the Universe is energy, and energy has a signature, a vibration. The Law of Attraction states that all energies like unto themselves will be attracted; it is the same for parents and prospective incoming souls. Each of you is a multidimensional being and you exist as a conscious being beyond the physical whilst you are present in the physical. Because your current focus and purpose is in the physical, you have only a vague recollection of what is non-physical. As a multidimensional, non-physical being, your consciousness spans many levels of consciousness. This span stretches from you at the cellular level right up to what you would term as 'God'. You could perhaps imagine yourself to be somewhat like a finger of God protruding into the physical realm. Your being is simultaneously present in the Physical, Astral, Mental, Christ, Buddhaic, all the multidimensional realities, including the Source. In essence, you have not left the Source; you have simply extended yourself outwards into another perspective of reality.

On each level of your being, you have a particular vibration. This vibration is determined by your emotional and mental make up; this composition is the sum total of all your experiences. Therefore, as you shift your focus once again towards the physical plane, you begin to align with all that exists on the physical plane which is in harmony with your own energy signature. If part of your total experience on Earth is that of poverty and your physical existences have been dominated by the thought that "life is always a struggle", then the prospective parents will be limited to those of a similar vibration, of similar thought patterns and beliefs. Additionally, souls are arranged into families, groups, clans, and nations, all multiples of seven. Souls generally work together on projects and will often have very similar goals, or goals that are compatible. In this way, a soul entering the physical who wishes to overcome poverty by creating great wealth is served by parents who offer a belief system that fulfils the general purpose of that soul.

We understand that it is very difficult for you to understand how a child can experience physical, sexual, or mental abuse and how these events can still be in harmony with the purposes of the soul. It is not that the personality has no freedom and that your soul can create for you circumstances that are beyond your control. Your inner being influences you with impulses and thoughts, with desires and with attraction to certain activities, thought forms, and people. However, whilst in the physical, the personality is very clearly in charge, and the soul seeks only to influence the actions of the personality through positive inspiration.

In the case of young children who have been abused, or who have debilitating and life-challenging diseases at a very young age, it serves you to remember that thought creates **all** conditions and that, from the time of conception, the forming child is strongly under the influence of the thoughts and beliefs of the parents and the family into which it is being born. Certain souls will also deliberately choose a physically challenging experience. The reasons for doing so are as numerous as the souls choosing to do so.

For example, one couple was focused only on the creation of wealth and the progress of their careers. This in itself is not a negative thing. However, they measured their value as people only through their income and their financial and social status. They both had difficulties in forming relationships and friendships, for their focus was almost entirely on the physical, even to the extent of judging others to be worthy or unworthy according to their social and financial standing. On a soul level, they had both been down this road before and had struggled with the issues for several lifetimes. At the soul level both of them felt that they were off track and needed a jolt to bring them back on track, for this aspect of their evolution was focused on bringing them to a place where they recognised inner wealth and, through tapping into their own inner wealth, they would then manifest outer wealth. Their goal was to create money and success through the exercise of love, through allowing. A soul that was in their soul group, a 'friend', came to them as a child through pregnancy. This child was born with several physical handicaps and was mentally handicapped too. The child required much love and attention, which was the entire objective of this birth. This child lived only for a short period of time, but it proved to be a powerful lifetime experience for both parents and child. The parents discovered their own capacity for love and selflessness and began to evaluate their self-worth in totally different ways. As for the incoming soul, it wanted to experience being 'helpless', for it had frequently experienced being an overachiever who rarely took any rest and also judged itself by performance. There was a vibrational match between the objectives of the three souls involved and each grew enormously through this experience. Even though the personalities involved may not be aware of the gifts presented within such experiences, on a deeper level there is always a profound change and the sense of knowing that all is right.

These examples are not intended to give you the impression that similar cases all occur for the same reason. Also, it is not to be surmised that souls get such 'lessons' because they have fallen short in some way. There is not some higher authority that decides what **you** must learn. You are the one that decides what you want to learn and how you want to learn it. Your primary purpose in coming to the Earth plane is to master all experience, so that you can manifest yourself in the physical as God, as the essence of love.

*"There is not some higher authority that decides what **you** must learn.*
You are the one that decides what you want to learn
and how you want to learn it."

All life is evolving, and as your species evolves, the ways in which you choose to learn also evolve. Therefore, the way in which you chose to learn several lifetimes ago is not going to be the same way you choose to learn in this lifetime or in the next. Until now, humanity has largely chosen to use pain as the vehicle for learning. You have habitually used pain, for it was the best way you had found to steer yourself in the right direction. This way of learning has now evolved to another level. Pain is no longer the primary mode of learning; joy has become the new frequency.

> *"Pain is no longer the primary mode of learning;*
> *joy has become the new frequency."*

This can be seen in the vast amount of material that is now encouraging you to do what you love to do, a message that we also support and convey. You are now at a stage of evolution such that you are growing and discovering through the sensing of different levels of what feels good. You are following your joy and feeling its different levels. This is a major shift for humanity and will soon begin to influence your systems of education and guidance greatly, for now you will no longer be so attracted to rules-based life choices, but will increasingly seek those pathways that lead to inner fulfilment.

Are negative conditions necessary for growth?

Absolutely not! Negative conditions are, in the simplest sense, the result of your thinking. Think of positive things and they will be yours; think of negative things and they too will be yours.

> *"Think of positive things and they will be yours; think of*
> *negative things and they too will be yours."*

Because the physical reality is characterised by the sense of 'not knowing', a sense of alienation from the All-That-Is, souls have used negative conditions to encourage the personalities they have created to move forward towards a more joyful experience. The physical reality is a perfect reality for feeling and experiencing comparison. In the physical reality, to experience a whole lot of what you don't want stimulates you into thinking about, and striving for, what you do want. Your primary intention, and this is true for all of you on the planet, is to create a life that fully expresses the four principles of creation mentioned above. You have deliberately set out to create a life in which you can express yourself in health and well-being, in abundance, and through love, and you do so by using your power to create. Comparison has helped you to experience yourself as what love is not, as what health is not, as what abundance is not.

This state of opposites seeks to catapult you forward. At any time you have the freedom to choose the positive pole of all that exists; there is no law or condition other than your own thinking that keeps you experiencing what is not joyful to you. Negative conditions are a choice, although we understand that you are not deliberately choosing them, but it is in giving your attention to them that renders them a choice in terms of the Universe responding to focus.

How can we transform negative conditions into positive ones?

Let us first be clear on the definition of negative conditions. A negative condition is anything you **perceive** as lacking in joyful experience for yourself. What I mean is that one person working at a bank may experience that function as being tedious and lacking in joy, therefore it is a negative condition for that personality. Another person may **perceive** that experience to be joyful and a definitely positive condition. Conditions are relative, for in essence, there is no reality, but simply your perception of it. All is relative.

For one person, living abundantly would mean living in a mansion with 16 bedrooms and a swimming pool, for another, living in a log cabin on the side of a beautiful mountain. The wealthiest person in one neighbourhood could be the poorest in another neighbourhood. This state of comparison may lead them to perceive themselves differently. In others words, their income may have remained static, but comparison leads them to certain perceptions of themselves. It is not conditions that are negative, but your perception of them.

We also understand your question here. You want to say something like, "How could I possibly change my perception of being robbed, raped, or murdered? They are definitely negative conditions; how could they be otherwise?" From the perspective of the personality in the physical dimension, they are indeed negative conditions. However, viewed from the perspective of the non-physical world, the co-creation of such events are as 'perfect' as the creation of health, wealth, or any other condition. The Universe responds to thought. From our perspective, we can view such an event as an opportunity for the personality to learn through the experience. The vision that we hold is that you should learn that you can create equally powerful experiences that you will find uplifting and joyful. Each event in your life, whether you perceive it to be positive or negative, is indeed divine grace in action. Each creation, each event, seeks to return you to the essence of who you are, to return you to love.

You can choose to shift your perception of a negative condition by seeking the gift of wisdom within it. For example, a soul that wishes to develop the quality of perseverance will most likely set up childhood conditions that will give the emerging personality beliefs that will be limiting, beliefs that perhaps lead to feelings such as 'there's no point', etc. With these sets of beliefs, and the inner impulse of the soul to move on and persevere, the personality will be driven to overcome its 'inadequacy'. The beliefs, because they are magnetic, will draw to the personality events that would appear to be stumbling blocks. However, in reality, they are gifts through which the soul is encouraging the personality to overcome the challenges and excel in developing the chosen pre-selected qualities.

None of this means that your soul produces the negative conditions, or that you are subject to the will of your soul. This is your life; you are in charge. However, the key to all of this is to be in contact with your feelings. It is through your feelings that your soul encourages you and guides you away from that which is less joyful. Your Soul, or Greater Self, is in contact with you moment by moment through your feelings. It was agreed that, as you emerged into this physical world, these lines of communication would be maintained.

What about negative conditions such as wars and natural disasters? Can we change those when in the midst of them? And why do they occur?

Let us first deal with the negative condition you call war. First, we must talk about mass consciousness and belief systems. Each nation, each ethnic grouping, each religious grouping, indeed, each region of the planet that identifies itself as being unique or different in some way, constitutes a collective consciousness. Nations, in those terms, are simply belief systems. Religious practices are a wonderful demonstration of this truth. For example, it is highly improbable in your system that a rice farmer from China or Thailand is going to be raised in the 'Christian' tradition, but rather in another belief system, be that religious or political. Therefore, the practice of religion has little to do with fact, or with what is correct, but has more to do with the prevailing beliefs of the region and culture into which you are born. Have you not acknowledged that what offends one person in one country is viewed as being innocuous in another land and vice versa? This has all to do with belief.

Beliefs are very powerful, and beliefs held by many form a belief system. When a sufficiently large group comes together to form a cohesive expression of that belief system, then a culture or nation is born. All of your nations are belief systems. Beliefs are thoughts that have been thought many, many times, and most of you give them great power. It is not so much that the beliefs in themselves wield such power, but that you believe strongly in your beliefs, in your 'cultural' identity, in what makes you 'different' from others, and what makes you 'belong' to your own group. Because you have a need to 'belong' and find acceptance within your own particular belief system, you will have the tendency to defend your beliefs vigorously.

War is not necessary, but it is also not wrong. It has become part of the human experience. Wars come about to facilitate change. It is often difficult for an individual to make radical changes in a belief system, and it is the same with large groups or a nation. However, if a deep-seated desire for change exists within a culture, then change will come about. Many of these desires for change go unspoken, but they do become part of the thread of the evolving culture. In our observation of humanity, we have seen that you have rarely, if ever, brought about change in ways that are easy and simple. As a species you have hitherto chosen to expand through pain and suffering. This concept of pain and suffering leading to 'salvation' can clearly be seen in many of your religious teachings.

In the simplest terms, groups create war as a way to promote change. You only need to look at how the cultures that were involved in World Wars I and II have evolved since those events.

Because you ask how you can change the negative situation whilst still in the midst of it, we ask you: How do you want to feel? When you make a clear statement of intention about how you want to feel, you will begin to perceive your physical conditions quite differently. According to the Law of Attraction, it is not possible for you to find yourself suddenly in the midst of a war or an earthquake or some other condition perceived to be negative unless you have a resonance or vibrational match with the situation. If you had been deliberately creating your life, deliberately each day or week setting your intentions towards abundance, peace, prosperity, safety, and joy, you would automatically be led away from such situations prior to their manifestation in your life. They are in your life because you have participated in their creation, irrespective of how unconscious that may seem. As a species, each of you is linked to one another. With this telepathic link, banks of thought are created; they are like clouds in which you exist, to use an analogy. These banks of thought become the overall 'feeling' or thought pattern of a culture and whether you are conscious of it or not, you begin to think just as the majority does.

Let us give you an example. There is an economic boom. Employment is up, inflation is down, sales are up, and all is rosy for your government, region, and country. As soon as the boom reaches its peak, 'analysts' and 'experts' begin to say that it cannot last long, or they ask, "When will the bubble burst?" This thought originates from the belief that all that is good is too good to be true; it comes from your collective beliefs in lack, struggle, and poverty. As soon as the 'this is to good to be true' thought is launched into the mass arena, the conditions are set for the arrival of the next financial slump or depression.

The same is true of the opposite case. As soon as things start getting really bad, and unemployment increases to a level never before reached and interest rates are sky high, some say, "We are about to turn the corner, it can't get worse." And there you have it, it can't get worse, so what happens? It starts getting better because your belief that it can't get worse launches new thoughts such as, "It must get better." This is a shift in focus, from lack to increase. As you accept that it can't get worse, you automatically begin thinking en masse that it can only get better, and so it does. The better it gets, the better it gets; the worse it gets, the worse it gets. In the same way that you have decided to limit things getting worse, you simply make the same decision regarding things getting better. Be unlimited in your thinking! Yes, a good thing can get better and better and can last forever!

Financial booms and depressions are a very good example for us to use when explaining mass reality to you because we are certain that these times of great financial swings have no logical sense for you. If the crops fail, you have a reason, but if they don't, and the recession comes along anyway, you don't have a reason that you can call logical. It is in this same way that you become a participator in a war, just as you participate in an economic recession. You are surrounded by media and by telepathic thought and by attention directed to the subject. Having said this, you are not subject to this telepathic influence if you **choose** not to be.

For the most part, the majority of you have forgotten that you are creators. You simply allow life to happen to you and you have become reactive beings instead of creative, pro-active beings. If you were to set a clear intention towards enjoying a joyful, healthful, abundant life each morning as you emerge into your reality, that is exactly what you would experience.

However, we also understand that at times it is too late, you are in the middle of the soup, and you wonder whether you are going to drown. This is when you use your ability to deliberately create your experience by stating your intention. Yes, you may be surrounded by mayhem, by the after effects of an earthquake or the threat of war or violence, in which case you set the same intention. Awaken in the morning and greet life with a smile and say out loud, "Today I intend to see all that is good in people and in life. Today I intend to see abundance." As you do this, even in the midst of a war or some other disaster, events and opportunities that show just these things will be drawn to you. You will see neighbours who have not spoken to each other for years helping one another. You will see courage, charity, and compassion, all that is good about human beings. You see, my beloved friends, there is no such thing as reality, there is only your perception of it.

"There is no such thing as reality,
there is only your perception of it."

One person can change the world, and was not it once said by the Master, "If you have faith the size of a mustard seed and command the mountain to move, it will move"? Indeed, you can move mountains, just believe that you can, focus only on the desired result, and the result will be yours.

Chapter 10

Sexual Behaviour

Can you give us guidelines on appropriate sexual behaviour?

Ah, this is a question that we delight in answering, for so many of you are concerned about it. It is not surprising that it is in the forefront of your mind, for sexual energy is what created the entire Universe, it is the creative force itself. It flows through your body during all the hours of your waking consciousness, it is with you, and it is part of you.

There are so many beliefs concerning sexuality, and we seek to answer this question fully. So make yourself comfortable, for there is much to say on the subject. First, we would apply the same advice to sexuality as to any other topic you are asking about, and that is to say: If it feels good, do it!

We already hear your voices saying "What about the rapists?" and "What about the child molesters?", and our answer to you is, they are not doing what feels good. They are doing what they feel compelled to do from a point of powerlessness and pain. This also applies to the sexual addict who seeks power and a sense of self-worth through sexual encounters. Sexuality is a medium through which you can share the sense of empowerment and self-worth, not gain it. Therefore, when we say, "If it feels good, do it," we mean exactly what we are saying. So many of you do not feel good at all and will use sexuality as a means for feeling good. Sex is just like any relationship; it is there to enhance your experience of yourself, not to give you something that you feel that you lack. What we mean by enhancing your experience of yourself, is that sexual union can lead you to an experience of great acceptance of another, of great love for another, of great joy in another. In this sense you experience being in acceptance, being love, being joyful appreciation, and therefore it enhances the experience of yourself and leads to growth.

What most of you are concerned about are the 'rules' pertaining to sexual union, for many of your religious traditions have handed down to you rules concerning sexual conduct. Cultures and people generally do what works for them, and although not necessarily joyful, the rules work to preserve order and circumnavigate difficulties. In order to understand the rules of a culture, it is important for you to understand the conditions under which the culture has developed and the underlying core beliefs of that culture.

Your religious rules and regulations were developed at a time when humanity was largely in survival mode. Great emphasis was placed on survival and the most time was spent in taking care of physical needs, in other words, acquiring food, shelter and clothing. All your questions about any subject must be placed within the context of human development. Just as you, as an individual, have had many, many lifetime experiences, cultures also undergo transformation, as is evident from viewing your history.

When a soul first comes into the physical world, it is trying to understand and cope with its new surroundings. It spends most of its time in survival mode, being very fearful of the physical world and its perceived threats. As the soul progresses, it becomes more accustomed to the physical world and attempts to build structures around itself so that the world becomes more manageable and less threatening. The vast majority of your 'moral' rules were developed in just such a period when humanity was creating structure in the world. This structure came in two forms, religions and also hierarchical societies that were shepherded by one or two families, in other words, chieftains and a royal class.

As cultures began to form, the natural biological differences between men and women became formalized within societal structures. In most of the cultures that eventually became dominant, men were expected to hunt, wage war, plough the fields, build structures and the like, and women were expected to tend to the needs of the men and fulfil their biological function of child bearer. Humanity has viewed itself as being separate or indeed 'superior' to the animal kingdom, but your social organisation has evolved along the same lines of fulfilling biological needs as have the animals. You are spiritual beings occupying a biological organism, and this organism has its own separate consciousness which is instinctive. You have a dual consciousness, instinctive and spiritual. Each species has the instinct to survive, to propagate, and to flourish and it does this by organising different roles for the sexes. As thinking human beings, your ability to organise is complex. However, the nature of that organisation is based on biological survival.

As the roles became more clearly defined, they became interwoven into religious and philosophical tradition. What was originally a biological impulse to survive and to flourish suddenly became a command from 'God'. As women were the nurturers and not the producers, they were on the one hand a financial burden to any family, but on the other hand a precious cargo, for they carried the ability to bear offspring. Out of this grew the tradition of offering a dowry to the family of any male who wished to take a female as a mate. The family of the female was literally compensating the family of the male for adding to their 'burden' with a 'non-productive' extra mouth to feed, for a woman did not fight wars, did not till the soil, did not build ships, and did not make other implements. Therefore, as women were excluded from taking on male roles, the culture needed to ensure that females were taken care of and did not become a burden. It is for this reason, and for this reason only, that sex before marriage was discouraged. The family of the female could not risk their daughters getting pregnant without a man to help support their needs. This would have created chaos and imbalance in cultures that were largely concerned with survival.

In order to consolidate this cultural necessity, it was then interwoven into religious tradition and elevated to the status of a 'command from God'. From an anthropological point of view, the rules concerning premarital sex made perfect sense.

Let us touch on another subject, the subject of homosexuality. This too became taboo, although there were always exceptions. In the times when such rules were developed, the cultures were tribal, as we have said. Often these tribes were surrounded by hostile neighbours. They competed for hunting grounds, competed for water, and competed for all and any resources. What guaranteed the success of any tribe were sheer numbers and sufficient males of fighting age and capability. Therefore from a biological standpoint, it was important that each male produce offspring and contribute to the gene pool of the tribe. It was for this reason that polygamy often existed in ancient civilisations, because it fulfilled that biological need.

What is important to understand here is the context within which societal rules were formed. Religion played a major role in holding together the cohesiveness of tribes and nations. Rules that made sense from the point of view of survival of the species, taking into consideration their focus and perception of reality, quickly became commands from 'God'. It was only 'God', by demanding obedience, who could curtail or suppress the natural biological inclinations.

These rules have been a part of your culture for so long that they are deeply embedded in your psyche. This is the reason why, since what you have termed the 'sexual revolution', there appears to be a preponderance of sexually transmitted diseases. It is not that the chosen behaviour is 'wrong', but that 'the disease' is created by your conflicting beliefs concerning appropriate sexual conduct.

Is there any sexual behaviour that is wrong?

We cannot use the term 'wrong', for in essence, all experience is relevant to the growth of the individual soul. However, there is that which is appropriate and that which is inappropriate. We would state very clearly that all activity that involves more than one being, whether sexual or not, should be consensual. In other words, it is inappropriate to involve anyone in activities that are not in accordance with their own free and chosen will, or whose personality is not in a position to make a clear and mature choice. Sexual abuse is always about powerlessness, expressing itself through the need of one to dominate another.

As we have stated before, do that which makes you feel good, and do all that you do with awareness. If you are seeking sexual gratification in order to compensate for a feeling of emptiness, then in the long run, this is not appropriate behaviour for you, although of itself it is not wrong. It is not wrong because the action may very well lead you to uncover the deeper issues at hand, and this brings growth, and growth is what your soul seeks at all times.

Sexual union is a creation. We advise each of you not only to see it as a creation, but also to be conscious and aware of your choices. Set an intention for joy each time that you join as one with another. You have the opportunity to experience the other as they truly are, and to experience yourself in love as you make love. It truly is a very precious and beautiful gift that you have given yourselves. It makes no difference whether the two who join are of the same gender or of mixed genders, what matters are the intentions of the individuals involved.

Sexual energy is the most powerful force in the Universe. It is the life force, creative energy itself. Without it, you would not have a physical body, nor would you have a soul body, for all springs forth out of creative process.

Why are some people Gay or Lesbian, and why does a soul have this experience?

The reason for a preference towards same sex experience and relationships are as numerous as those who choose this experience. When we say choose, we do understand that from the point of view of the one with a same sex orientation that it is simply the way that they are, it is not a choice. However, when we refer to choice, we do so in the context of the eternal soul and its choice to add this experience to a broad panorama of experiences. It is useful to note two important things here. First, each soul that completes a cycle of lives on the Earth plane will choose at least one homosexual life. A life of same sex orientation provides a soul with unique opportunities for growth and experience that enriches its Earth adventure. The second thing to note here is that by nature, each of you is bisexual. This does not mean to say that this bisexuality necessarily needs to lead to sexual union with partners of both genders, but it means that each of you is capable of feeling great love for another human of the same gender and of expressing that in a physical way. Each individual's sexual orientation is unique and is expressed with differing emphases, meaning that one person could be almost exclusively heterosexual, and another person could be almost exclusively homosexual, but the majority of you fall somewhere between the two poles. Whether you act upon, or are even conscious of this bisexuality is a different question all together.

For many gay individuals, but not all, there is an association with the role of the opposite sex. This role identification takes place in the first seven years of life and is a pre-chosen set of circumstances prior to incarnation. A child will usually identify with the role of the parent of the same gender; a child's identification with the role of the opposite sex is likely to lead to homosexual preference being expressed and chosen as a lifestyle. What is really important here is not to analyse why something is, but to understand the value of such an orientation from the point of view of the soul.

As clearly stated above, such orientations are a necessary part of soul development, for they offer many opportunities for growth and development. Once could say that it is an exalted role, for it provides the individual soul with unique challenges that strengthen and assist the soul to achieve its long-term goals. The long-term goal of any soul is to find self-acceptance whilst in physical form. Self-acceptance leads to love, compassion, courage, generosity, sacrifice, and gratitude, all the qualities that the soul wishes to develop and express.

Living a gay lifestyle offers opportunities for self-examination that other roles do not. First, because your culture has largely feared and mistrusted its own sexuality, it has feared and misunderstood same sex orientation. This has created an atmosphere of discrimination, even persecution. This in itself is sufficient to motivate some souls to want to have that experience, for it has the potential to catapult the soul forward in its growth. You see, the soul always seeks growth, you are growth-seeking beings. So, from the soul's perspective, if it wants to develop courage or self-acceptance, it may very well choose a same sex oriented life for that purpose.

Gay and lesbian lives are always about growth and are generally chosen by more mature and older souls in order to further their advancement. The self and discovery of the self are the keys to all spiritual growth. As a member of a sexual minority, these individuals, when young, are naturally drawn to ask themselves, "Who am I?" and, "Why am I different?" much earlier than those who are members of a majority. Heterosexual individuals very rarely question their sexuality; they simply accept that they are the way they are. In addition to this, the relationship with parents plays a key role in terms of offering the growth sought by the individual soul. Each of you gains your sense of self-worth and value largely from your relationship with those who 'created' you. Often, depending on the culture, many same sex oriented individuals experience either outright rejection or distance from their 'creators'. This is a source of great pain for these individuals. However, it brings the opportunity to find that self-worth does not come from 'pleasing the creator' but comes from within. It springs forth from self-appreciation.

The vast majority of you still imagine that there is an external God that you need to please or whose approval you need to win. You put much emphasis on trying to find out what this God wants of you. This, for the most part, is a direct transference of your relationship with one or both parents onto the imagined God. A gay individual is being provided with all the circumstances that will assist him or her to find their true source of love, power and self-worth in themselves. This is also aided by the fact that children will seldom play a role in gay relationships. Most of you, as you get older, see your life as being fulfilled through children. You have fulfilled your 'duty' to the species by reproducing, and you are being fulfilled in other ways through parenting and grandparenting. The lack of these roles gives the soul even more opportunity for more self-exploration, for everything must come from within.

A gay life is a very valuable life that calls upon many inner resources and provides many opportunities for spiritual enlightenment. There are many ways to accomplish this; there are simpler ways, and there are more challenging ways. A gay or lesbian life is an exalted role that is chosen for growth. For this reason, many gay men and women in your culture are ideally suited to the roles of counselling, healing, nursing, care, and spiritual teaching.

Why does pornography exist, and what is a healthy relationship to it?

This is a large and complex subject and we could answer from many, many different angles. However, to keep things as simple as possible, we offer to you that pornography is filling the needs of those who do not feel that they are able to or 'allowed' to express themselves sexually. Those who view such material on a regular basis feel that they are lacking in some way. Either they have a mate with whom they feel they are unable to express themselves fully, or they have suppressed their natural desires and inclinations and seek a way to express them. Sexual energy is the most powerful force in the Universe. It is with you and runs through you all continuously. However, for the historical reasons we have already discussed, it has become a taboo subject and an energy that many fear.

Whenever any naturally occurring energy becomes suppressed, it will always manifest in some dysfunctional way. However, that is not to say that pornography is a 'dysfunction'. Like anything, it all depends on your intention and motivation. For example, pornography can be used as an educative tool for those who wish to broaden their experience. It can also be appreciated as an art form, or be celebrated as an expression of life force energy. However, in our observation, the majority of viewers use such materials from a position of lack, rather from a position of celebrating and honouring human sexuality. There is no wrong or right with pornography, it is how you use it that makes a difference in your life.

You spoke earlier of a gay lifestyle being a necessary role for the soul to choose as part of its journey through many lifetimes here on Earth. Are there any other roles that we must all play as part of the Earth experience?

Indeed, yes, there are. We call them the four P's. These four roles are archetypes and are not always literal. The roles are: Prince, Pauper, Priest, and Prostitute.

The Prince and Pauper roles are all to do with power, how it is expressed and the responsibility that goes with such power. As opposites, a soul will choose lives that have financial and/or political power, or lives that are completely devoid of both. The soul seeks to experience these opposites so that the subject matter can be fully understood.

The roles of Priest and Prostitute are all about both conditional and unconditional service. Elements of power enter into both these roles as well, but on the whole, the general lesson is about service. Unconditional service can be learned and experienced in either role, just as conditional service can be expressed in either role.

These four roles are pivotal to any soul's development and growth, because they provide unique challenges. As archetypes, the literal role is not always chosen. However, the majority of souls do choose the literal role at least once. In the case of a Prince, this is anyone that has cultural status and influence. In the case of a priest, that is any role that administers to the spiritual needs of the culture, whether formally or informally. Examples of the priestly role are medicine men and women, therapists, counsellors, priests, shamans, and psychics. The role of pauper is anyone in a position that appears to lack choice. This role is widespread and can be witnessed amongst those belonging to racial minorities and those who are dominated by external authorities such as religions and governments. The prostitute is a role that the soul more often chooses literally, and like the priest, it is about learning the differences between conditional and unconditional service.

In essence, all the roles assist souls to understand power and how to use it. Priests and prostitutes alike can gain a false sense of power over their 'clients' through the need for their services that the 'client' expresses. Princes and Paupers are also primarily occupied with the gaining of power and the exercise of it. Those of you who identify with the role of Priest will have often experienced the role of Prostitute; the two go hand in hand. Those who identify with the role of Prince will likewise have experienced many lifetimes as a Pauper.

What these roles are all about is the exercise of personal power. True power comes from within and does not seek to dominate or control any other being. False power, power that is based on feelings of lack, always involves manipulation and contains a sense of 'power over', even if this is subtle. As you become increasingly more aware of your non-physical self, you become increasingly more powerful. One who is fully blended with source and is in the physical dimension is able to wield great power, indeed, is able to move mountains, for this one knows that matter is energy, just as all is energy. This knowing enables the blended one to manipulate all matter with thought, for this one understands that he or she is at one with the power that created all worlds. Therefore, the roles we have described are a necessary foundation for the cultivation of such power.

There have been cultures on your planet that were highly advanced, and many individuals within those cultures could perform what you would term miracles. They could manipulate matter, move heavy objects with their minds, and had great command over the weather and other elements, for they knew that as they thought, so it was. However, there were many instances of individuals, and indeed entire groups of beings, that abused their power for personal gain and gratification, for they became fascinated with the power. There are so many of you who have had these very experiences in other lifetimes that you are spending hundreds of lifetimes in this cycle to bring your relationship with power into balance.

Power is a wonderful thing; it is who you are. You are all such powerful and wonderful beings. However, to be useful, power is to be channelled through the heart. Otherwise, it creates forms that are temporary, for anything based on lack is but a temporary illusion.

Chapter 11

Which Information is Worthy of Our Attention?

There is so much information that is available to us and so many sources who are claiming to be non-physical like yourself, Omni. How can we tell which information is worthy of our attention?

Did not a great Master say "By their fruits ye shall know them?" How does the information make you feel? Without the presence of inner guidance, all guidance that comes from outside you is of little use. When you understand the nature of inner guidance, you will automatically know truth when you hear it and see it.

All true guidance comes from within and although we are a group of non-physical beings that have conspired together to communicate our broader vision through this channel, we could not do so unless this one's inner self was fully present at the times of our communication. So how does inner guidance feel? Inner guidance never warns. It does not frighten you nor tell you of impending doom or gloom, and it does not flatter you. Your soul seeks to uplift you and to guide you into discovering more of who you are. It does not set you apart, it is not jealous, it is not fearful, it does not scheme or gossip, nor warn you against others. Also, it does not claim to be your saviour, for it seeks to teach you that you are the master of your own destiny and that your will is dominant in this physical place.

"All true guidance comes from within."

Much information is coming forth from the non-physical world. Just as there are frivolous individuals and individuals that seek to control or mislead you in the physical world, there are those in the non-physical who seek to mislead or control you who are, or are simply seeking entertainment. Like everything in your world, all you draw to yourself is the result of your thoughts and intentions regarding the subject.

If you seek that which uplifts and inspires you, it will come. If you seek that which helps you understand who you truly are, it will come. If you seek that which helps you understand the Universe and how its laws work, that too will come to you. Everything works according to the Law of Attraction; that which you think of will be drawn unto you.

As a species, you have only recently begun to move away from the concept that there is a God outside of you that has wishes for you and makes demands of you, and is responsible for your salvation. With thoughts like these deeply embedded in your consciousness, it is logical that beings that fit this picture of the Universe will be drawn to some and will tell stories of the fight between good and evil. They will tell stories of doom and gloom and impending natural and other disasters. Or other beings may be attracted that suggest that 'if you don't do this or that, your life will be miserable', or similar things. These beings exist, for some of you have drawn them into their experience through the beliefs they are holding.

Sometimes, the being that is channelled is not non-physical at all, but the subconscious mind of the individual concerned. This is not necessarily bad, for much good information can come from human consciousness!

Whatever the source and whatever the claim, ask yourself these questions. Does the teaching hold a positive vision for humanity? Does the teaching remind me of who I truly am and encourage me to be all I can be? Does the teaching encourage me to be allowing and accepting of all? Does the teaching engender unconditional love? Does the teaching assist me to feel good about myself without resorting to flattery? Does the teaching encourage forgiveness and understanding of others? Does the teaching emphasize your free will to choose, or does it claim to be the only source?

There are many sources of good, channelled information available to you, but some of it will not appeal to you and some of it will greatly elevate and inspire you. Not all teachers come for all students. Each teacher springs forth to teach those who are of similar vibration. We come forth to reach those who are looking for the information we have to share. What we offer you is our unique perspective based upon the collective experience of our entire group of beings. This collective experience is unique in the Universe, for no other group has had precisely our range of experience. This uniqueness adds to the richness of the Universe and adds to the richness of teaching. What we teach is not unique, for Universal truths are constant. However, our flavour, if you like, is unique. We are travellers, communicators with many species on many physical worlds, teachers in what you call your astral plane and on other planes of existence. We offer you our perspective, and do so with love.

Your natural inner guidance teaches and directs you with love. As you ask for guidance, it will be offered to you. You can always know when you are in alignment with your inner guidance—you will feel good. Remember, emotions and feelings are the tools that your Inner Self, your soul, uses to guide you. When you feel good, it is your soul saying, "Yes, think more like this, do more like that," and when you feel bad it is your soul saying, "What you are currently thinking and doing is not in harmony with your greater purpose." As you ask for guidance, it will be given to you. It may come in a dream, as direct inspiration, via the words of a friend, or via a book. As you read this book, you will sense your Inner Self encouraging you to absorb some pieces of information more than others. You will feel good reading some parts and neutral when reading other parts. When you feel good, it is your inner guidance working for you, encouraging you to embrace the ideas presented to you. Other parts of any book or teaching will stimulate you mentally, and that is also fine, for you do need to satisfy the needs of your logical mind.

"Your natural inner guidance
teaches and directs you with love."

Everything that springs forth from spirit will convey love and substance. Remember this, my beloved friends, you are the highest authority in your life, no other! There is no one that knows what is best for you better than you do. There is no one that knows the truth of who you are better than you do. We seek only to remind you of that which you have told yourself that you have forgotten. But you have known these things all along, and we come to celebrate with you and tell you that we are you, for we are that which you aspire to be, and you are that which we have been. As we communicate with humanity, the inner selves of all those that we come into contact with conspire with us to send you these messages and teachings. All that we offer is the teaching of your own inner self, your own soul. That is why we can say, "We are you," for that is how we experience our reality.

"Everything that springs forth from spirit
will convey love and substance."

How do you feel about the Ouija board? Is it safe? Is it valuable?

The determination of whether something is safe and useful, or otherwise, is dependent upon your intention. The Ouija board is well known in certain non-physical realms as a game, and there are non-physical beings that like to use it as such. If you sit at a board and have no further intention than to attract that which is non-physical, then indeed, you will attract that which is non-physical.

Just because an intelligence is non-physical, that does not make it wise or helpful! Such beings do indeed have a slightly broader view. They dwell in what you call your astral plane, largely populated by what you would refer to as your 'dead' ones. These beings can win your confidence through giving you information of which you can have no knowledge, but which is verifiable, such as a prediction of sorts. The astral world is beyond time as you know it, and therefore such information is available to beings there. And, not all beings focused in the astral plane are frivolous or out to deceive you. There are indeed some very high beings on that plane, beings that have either 'travelled' to the astral plane to serve as guides and teachers for those in that focus, or souls who have completed all of their physical lifetimes on Earth and remain in the astral plane to serve members of their Soul Group who are still physical.

When using tools such as the Ouija board, set a clear and determined intention. Bless your time with the board, call upon the light, and summon forth all that which is loving and wise in the Universe, asking that only the highest teacher guides make themselves known. And be *specific* about the information you wish to receive. The Law of Attraction is all-pervading, and you will attract to yourself the object of your attention. If you seek that which uplifts you, educates you for a higher path, assists you to know more about yourself, then you will enjoy rewarding sessions with the Ouija board.

If you go to the board without a clear intention, then you will attract that which is unclear. Likewise, if you go to the board with fears, having heard stories of things that go bump in the night, you will likely attract those 'bumps in the night' and that which is frivolous. Remember that you are a sovereign being, and your word is law. If any being, no matter who or what it claims to be, begins telling you that you *must* do as it says, or that its truth is higher and better than yours, that one is not coming from a high plane of existence. Use your discernment. Many see the Ouija as a game; it certainly is not. You can use it to gain good information and to grow.

Also remember that the Ouija board is only a tool, just like the pendulum, or the tarot cards. All true wisdom comes from within. Although we encourage you to use such tools with a clear intention towards growth, we encourage you to go within and seek your guidance there. Perhaps the Ouija board can be a stepping-stone for you; it is your decision.

Do we need to guard against negative entities or demonic forces?

Absolutely not! That does not mean there are no negatively oriented beings in the Universe, for there are. However, we remind you of the Law of Attraction. The Universe delivers unto you that to which you are directing your attention. If you believe you need to be protected, then indeed you will need to protect yourself. If you believe that negative entities can harm you or influence you, then they will.

Be clear in your intention. If you seek contact with the non-physical, ask for that to come forth which exists in a state of unconditional love, ask for that to come forth which lives in a state of wisdom and bliss, ask for that to come forth which has the greater good of all, and it will. Spend time protecting yourself against that which is 'evil' and you will become like a magnet for that energy! Give it no attention, and it won't be yours; give it attention, and it will be yours. The Universe does not respond differently to 'I want' and 'I don't want'; it simply responds to attention.

Who and what are spirit guides?

Spirit guides are as varied as the members of your own species, and more so! A spirit guide can be a relative that has passed out of the physical and now seeks to guide you through the rest of your physical life. These guides will always be members of your Soul Group and you will have known them for many lifetimes. They may be complete with their Earth experiences and therefore choose to serve as a guide before moving into other dimensions and realities. Although you may experience them as the personality you knew whilst they were in the physical, it is indeed their Greater Self, their soul, with its broader, greater perspective, that is acting as the guide. They will retain the outer clothing of their personality-self so that you may identify with them.

This is also true of other guides that come forth from your Soul Group. Perhaps you knew them in a past life, perhaps sharing a life in an ancient or foreign culture. In this case, they may choose to appear to you as a member of that historical culture because it is known to you on a deeper level and engenders feelings of trust.

Spirit guides can be members of your own Soul Group or indeed aspects of yourself. You see, you are a vast being in your own right. As this being, you have had many thousands of lifetime experiences and you have a lot to offer yourself in terms of wisdom and experience. Your Higher Self often appears to you as a guide. All guides, whether they be a part of your Soul Group or not, work in cooperation with your Higher Self; it cannot be any other way. Your Soul, or Higher Self in this context, is the captain of the ship and guides you day and night.

There are other spirit guides that fall outside this category; these souls are perhaps far removed from your own Soul Group, but take an avid interest in the development and growth of humanity. They can be the souls of beings that are physically present on other planets, many, many light years away from your own, or they can be beings that have never been physical, perhaps coming through from a parallel Universe. No matter the guides or where they come from, there is always cooperation with your Higher Self before they communicate. Some guides, such as myself, are a collective, a group of beings that have grouped together in order to lend assistance through teaching whenever called upon.

As beings in the physical, you are seekers of answers. You want to know who you are, where you came from, and where you are going. We, the Beings of Light, are a response to that seeking. In essence, you invite your guides to come to you because you are seeking the answers that we are here to offer. We are indeed a product of your desire.

Some people claim to have received guidance from Jesus. Is that so?

Any being may communicate with any other being if there is sufficient desire to do so. Let us make a clear distinction between the soul of the man you know as Jesus, son of Joseph, and what is known collectively as the Christ. The Christ is a level of consciousness. It is an awareness and experience of oneness through the heart. It says, "I am at one with All-That-Is; All-That-Is is connected to me." Through meditative practice and your desire to grow spiritually, there are increasing numbers of you today who have been able to reach this level of consciousness, both during meditative practice and at other times spontaneously.

Often, as humans are apt to do, when this level of consciousness is reached in meditation, you interpret that encounter as an encounter with the one called Jesus. This occurs because the energy that you sense is recognisable; you know it. Because you are aware that Jesus, son of Joseph, was one whom embodied this energy, your human mind will interpret it in that fashion, giving it a form so that it is more tangible and interpretable for you. However, the soul that became the man Jesus of Nazareth, and later the Christ, does indeed make contact with many beings.

From our point of view and from the point of view of Jesus, once you reach the level of this consciousness, the level of oneness, it really does not matter, for at that instant you are united with all at this level. So yes, there are those through whom Jesus speaks, there are those through whom the Christ speaks, there are those through whom Gautama Buddha speaks, there are those through whom 'God' speaks, and there those through whom we speak. Each communication will carry its unique signature, depending on the individual through whom the communication is coming. We may not even identify ourselves by name, or we may simply give you a name to satisfy your human need for identification. Remember this, God seeks to remind you that you are loved. If we will get your attention by calling ourselves Jesus, then we will. If calling ourselves Fred will give us more credibility, then we will use that name. Names are for humans; we simply are.

What we really hear in your question is this: "If one, speaking through another, is representing himself as Jesus or any other, how can we know if that is for real?" Our answer is simple: Does the messenger convey, "I am at one with All-That-Is, All-That-Is is connected to me?" Is there substance to what is being said, and is the pervading energy one of love, acceptance, and allowing? If it is, then listen; if it is not, move on and find a teacher that does speak to your heart.

Jesus, the Buddha, and many others are present to serve humanity. You can call upon them for their light, love, wisdom, and guidance whenever you wish to. As you ask for it, so it is yours!

Many people are talking about Ascension, a time when we can take our physical bodies with us into the non-physical, as if this will happen very soon or on a particular given date. What does all this mean from your perspective?

Let us say that we prefer the word Descension, for that is your purpose for being on the planet. What was your purpose for coming here? Did you not come here to know that you are God? We have referred many times to the age of souls, talking of old souls, mature souls, new souls, etc. Although more often than not this refers to the number of Earth lifetime experiences an individual soul has had, it is not necessarily always so. A soul can mature and become an old soul rapidly, or proceed at a snail's pace, over many, many hundreds of physical lifetime experiences. What distinguishes an old soul from a young soul is the presence and influence of the Soul, the Greater Self, upon the personality. When the soul is present and influencing the personality, the life of that individual takes on a greater meaning. He or she begins to see purpose and design behind all experiences in life, and takes on a broader spiritual perspective.

When you came into the physical, you decided that you would master this reality. To master this reality is to live in a state of total harmony with simultaneous and equal awareness of both your physical being and that which is non-physical. In this state, you can say with the Master, "I and the Father are one," for at this stage you will **know** that you are connected to all that is. This is what we mean when we speak of Descension.

Relatively few souls choose this path. Most of you choose to move beyond the Earth plane once you have achieved a lifetime or two where your soul is the captain of the ship and exerts great influence over your life. Many of you are at the beginning stages of this now. You are driven perhaps by a sense of purpose, and are keen to resolve inner issues and expand yourself to a state of allowing and acceptance of the world. There are also those who, once they have completed this stage, will return to the Earth for a special purpose. These souls, like the soul of Jesus, will then make themselves available for an even greater consciousness by becoming present on the planet for the purposes of uplifting and teaching humanity. This greater consciousness will 'take over' the personality that volunteered for this role at the soul level and will literally become 'God amongst humanity', for it will be the representation of Unity Consciousness, the All-That-Is in human form.

There are beings, and there have been a few on Earth, who are able to phase in and out of the physical world, taking on different physical bodies each time that they do so. There have also been beings born into a physical body that are able to move in and out of this reality; however, this is rare. Though, as more and more of you grow spiritually and the vibration of your world increases, this will become more common.

Your planet, just like yourselves, is a multidimensional being. Just as you have a personality self, a Higher Self, a Soul Self, and a formless self that we will call the monad, so does the Earth. Your planet is the product of the collective consciousness of all that inhabits the world. Just as there are many versions of you, there are many versions of the Earth. There is an Earth that inhabits the same 'space' as does your Earth but at a different frequency. In fact, there are several of these. Your physical Earth, as you experience it today, can be likened to the personality self, a self that is still largely bound by illusion but is beginning to get an inkling of a greater, higher truth. There is also the Higher-Self version of the Earth; this is the version that you are in the process of phasing in with at the moment. The Higher-Self Earth still looks and feels very much like the personality-self Earth. The main difference is that the Soul-Self Earth is exerting great influence upon it. It looks and feels like the Earth, but the collective vision and purpose is consciously focused on upward growth. Then there is the Soul-Self version of Earth. This Earth is the shepherd of all the other versions of your world in their multidimensions. Here your souls are gathered together and transmit higher ideals to all its other versions. All consciousness is multi-faceted. We are like Shiva, many arms, and many faces. Just as your soul has many faces, so does your world.

Much of what you understand about Ascension is about shifting as a group away from your focus in the personality Earth towards the Higher-Self Earth. This process is gradual and goes on largely unnoticed. Sufficient time will pass and you will suddenly find yourselves in the new expression without having noticed that you have left the older expression. The personality-self Earth will last eons, as will the other expressions of the planet. Hundreds of cultures have come and gone at your level. All that is currently occurring has happened before. There is truly nothing new under the sun; everything follows cycles. Some have returned to repeat all that they have learned, and others have moved their vibration on to a different expression of your world. We do not see a mass shift that takes place on a particular date, but a gradual process that is gathering momentum.

The more you grow, the more you grow. In other words, growth is exponential. The more individuals in your world who shift their vibration upwards towards the vibration of love, the more others will be able to accomplish the same with less effort, and so on and so on, until critical mass is reached. Reaching this level will take more time than some have predicted—

not because things are going wrong, but simply because that is the nature of things. When you have eternity, there is no need to rush.

When we talk of Ascension, we talk of it not in terms of moving with your physical body, but we talk about the upward shifting of your consciousness. The consciousness of this planet has been very egocentric, concerned with exercising control over each other and over your environment. There has been a focus on intellectual abilities. The shift in the midst of which you currently find yourselves is a shift towards a greater awareness of your emotional body. This shift is evident in the media and many other forms of communication. You are exchanging and exploring human feelings and emotions.

Many of you may question the value of 'emotional TV'; however, you could see it as a form of cultural catharsis in which human relationships, drama, and emotions are played out on your television screens. As this shift is occurring, you are also experiencing the commonality that exists between you, experiencing that others feel as you do, have the same needs, experiences, fears, and wishes. This is leading to the realisation that you are in truth all one. This insight is leading to the opening of the heart centre of humanity. This is indeed the return of the Christ of which Jesus spoke. It is a collective experience which is about the opening of your collective and individual capacity to love. You see, beloved, the only measure of your spiritual growth is your capacity to love. When we speak of Ascension, this is what we refer to, your ability to ascend out of fear and upwards into love.

Chapter 12

Create Your Own Reality

When is it appropriate to tell one's children that they create their own reality?

When would **you** have liked to have been told? So, you learned when you were 35 and already a mother? Did you ever wish that you had known earlier? Yes, of course, you say, of course, for it would have helped you understand your life circumstances better. Our admonition is to tell your little ones as soon as they can talk. As you walk your talk, so will they. Speak to them of your own dreams and aspirations. As children grow up, most parenting is based on the idea of protecting them from dangers. You tell them not to speak to strangers, you tell them not to cross the road, you tell them not to touch what is dirty and to keep away from an open flame. Your way of educating them largely puts them in a defensive mode where they learn, as you have learned, how to resist the world and push against the things they don't want, just as you have been doing.

Would you deny anyone the valuable knowledge that they create their own reality? Then don't deny it to your children. When you inform your children about who they are, they will become your teachers and you will marvel at them. How much more appropriate it is to tell your child, "You are a child of the Universe and the power that creates worlds is within you. As you think of something you want, and focus for a little while on the nice feeling of possessing it, it will be yours," instead of, "Save for a rainy day, you never know when things may run out!"

You can become whatever you want to be, and most of you struggle with that concept. You believe it, or at least want to believe it; it sounds logical, but your inner feelings tell you otherwise for you have been programmed and taught to accept less. How grand it would be if you could give your children the gift of knowing, as they emerge into this world, that they can become whatever they want.

How can I balance what is practical with what I know to be true? For example, if I tell my children they can have, and do, and become whatever they want, how do I tell them that I can't afford to buy them the thing they are asking me for? I don't want to send them contradictory messages.

Remember, children are fickle beings, even more so than their parents! Just as we have taught you to feel what it is that you want, teach your own children the same thing. You are not teaching your child that the Universe will provide an ice-cream each time he or she asks for one, for you know that too much of that is inappropriate. First, teach your children how to feel, and if they want something big thing, tell them to keep it a secret and to play with their wishes for a while. You see, for the most part, a child's wishes are short lived. Little Tommy wants a new red bicycle, and he really believes that he wants it. Then just one day after deciding that he really, really wants it, he sees the other boys in the neighbourhood all have blue bicycles, so guess what? Tommy now wants a blue one, and no longer a red one. That is the nature of children. What we are teaching you is what we advise you to teach your children. You do not sit about and visualise buying a bunch of grapes, do you? No, for the means to do so is already within your realm of expectation. Your belief system has already delivered you to the point where no hurdles need to be overcome in order to acquire a bunch of grapes.

Teach your children, as we teach you, that they are the source of all that they want. Tell them that, if they change their mind each day, the Universe won't know what to send them. Let us say this to you. If a child really and truly wants a new red bicycle, and allows it into his or her life and gets to a point of expectation, it will come. Either you, or an uncle, aunt, grandparent, or a prize will deliver it to that child.

The disappointments that occur in a child's life are caused by the unspoken communication between parents and child. Every thought that you have as a parent is communicated directly to your child, whether or not that child is physically present. If you as the parent are struggling with self-worth, or finances, or a lack of self-confidence or respect, then those feelings are passed on to the child.

Every unresolved emotion gets passed on to the child. Every belief gets passed on to the child. Children are like sponges. The greatest service you can offer them is to change your beliefs concerning abundance. If you are afraid that your children's belief in abundance is going to be a drain on your resources, then this is a sign for you to change your own beliefs regarding your resources.

I have two children. One child I feel very close to. I recognised him the minute he was born; it was a close soul connection. I love my other child, too, but she has recognised this special connection and I sense that she feels left out or hurt.

You have a soul connection to both children, not just to the one child. No child is born to parents without there being an agreement and dialogue between the parents and the incoming soul. You may not be aware of this dialogue, but we assure you it was there.

Remember that each child came to you voluntarily and that you voluntarily agreed to be the host parent. You may or may not have had more lifetime connections with the one child, but that is relatively unimportant. Do not deny your feelings or your attraction to the one child, for this child is reflecting something back you. What might that be? Each child inherits imprinting that forms the basis of the personality. This imprinting is passed down from generation to generation. Perhaps this child reminds you of a parent or grandparent. Perhaps the feeling of preference for the one child is because the other child shows you an aspect of yourself that you have yet to resolve. It is far too simplistic to answer all these feelings of special connections with suggestions that imply past life and soul connections. When we observe humanity, we observe that most, if not all, things come forth from within the family dynamic, both from within your new family, and your original family.

Each child that comes into your life comes with a gift. They come to show you who you are through the experience of being a parent to them. This is indeed the greater gift of parenting. All souls within the same biological family come together consciously and out of choice in order to help one another grow. The best question you can ask is what are your children teaching you about yourself? In answering that question, you can begin to embrace parenting with a more open heart and see your children as emerging adults, emerging personalities that are on the same spiritual path as you.

"Each child that comes into your life comes with a gift."

I was born with a physical limitation and have come to accept this as 'karma' from a past life or as something that I choose to learn from in this life. However, how can I be assured that I don't take this condition with me and create a future life with the same problem?

Let us reassure you that what you call 'karma' has nothing to do with punishment or retribution for deeds done in past lives. Your thoughts and emotions are the cause of karmic conditions, and these thoughts and emotions can develop certain patterns over time.

When a child is born with a physical limitation, it always has to do with the family itself. Emotional entanglements and blockages arise within family units that can last for generation after generation, often passed through either the male line or the female line. An incident such as the loss of a child, sexual abuse, the early death of a parent, an adoption, or forms of repressive, oppressive, or restrictive behaviour, can all be passed from mother to daughter, to granddaughter, to great granddaughter, and likewise from father to son, and to grandsons. As almost all children associate emotionally with the parent of the same gender, to learn about that particular role, they also absorb the emotional blockages of the parent in question. This parent in turn may have taken on an emotional burden from the grandparent, and so on and so on. When you look at human families, you often see repetition. Often mothers who have children during their teens will have daughters who do the same. A child always seeks harmony, and when he or she observes a mother or father's pain, the child will often voluntarily take on part or most of the burden, out of love for the parent. This is the nature of children and the soul knew, prior to manifesting itself as the child, that this would occur.

The emotional entanglements literally block the flow of life force energy in the developing foetus. A foetus develops as a direct expression of the incoming soul. Each contour of the face, skull and body is an expression of the emotional state of the soul in question. So-called 'birth defects' are in fact the compounded effect of unresolved emotions within a given family.

However, the incoming soul is aware of this prior to incarnation, and the blueprint of its upcoming life is chosen consciously and with awareness. The incoming soul almost always has an intimate relationship with other members of the family, having worked with them in other incarnations or in the non-physical planes. However, at times a soul can volunteer to work with a family that is unknown to it in order to help them move forward. When it does so, the volunteer soul's evolution is also helped forward.

When your scientists speak of genetic defects or inherited illnesses, it is of this that they are speaking. It is consciousness that builds the body, and just as the great-great-grandmother's emotional state may have caused a physical ailment, this ailment can then be passed on to the descendants down the female line if there has been no resolution of the particular emotion, or the restrictive belief behind the emotion. Often, the very same soul that was the great-great-grandmother, for example, will re-enter the family as the great-great-granddaughter in an attempt to resolve the family issue. This occurs more frequently than is supposed.

So why would a soul choose an environment that it knows in advance may lead to physical or emotional challenges? You are all growth-seeking beings, and as such will take any opportunity to expand your capacity to love. Almost without exception, all the souls involved in such emotional entanglements are known to each other and have worked together as a biological family unit in previous lifetimes. Problems that occur in one generation are revisited in another as the souls involved seek to resolve all the problems in which they have taken part. If the original family 'karma' began with the great-grandfather who forced an unwed daughter to give up her child for adoption, then, if the inherited emotional state has not yet been resolved, that great-grandfather may choose to be reborn into the same family as the grandchild of the original daughter in order to do so.

As that soul approaches the physical plane of the family in question, just prior to incarnation, its vibration begins to change. It begins to resonate once again with the 'family karma', and the body it builds begins to reflect that vibration. A family's strongly held beliefs can also have similar effects. When a sperm and an egg come together, not only does the DNA combine to create a unique being, but also there is a unique preparatory aura formed around the newly created single cell. Each sperm carries a replica of the auric field of the father and each egg carries a replica of the auric field of the mother. In this magnetic energy field are contained all the emotions, thoughts, beliefs, wishes and hopes of the parent. As egg and sperm combine, all these thoughts and feelings combine to create a unique mental and emotional body for the incoming soul. To this energy field is added the unique energy signature of the incoming soul, if indeed a soul has chosen to incarnate at that time. The unique signature of the incoming soul will contain the totality of all that soul's experience. This soul energy, knowledge, and experience will fuse with the newly formed aura. In this way, a unique personality is created as a combination of mother, father, and incoming soul qualities.

If the mother of the incoming child had feelings of deep loneliness, these feelings would also become part of the child's experience. However, the child is under the strong influence of the soul. The soul may have chosen this particular mother because it, too, had struggled with loneliness in past life experiences, and therefore **chose** once again to take on this 'blueprint for life' from the mother in order to evolve through this feeling. This is how a soul seeks growth.

Whatever the situation, whatever the ailment or physical limitation, or even mental illness, it is essential to remember that all this is done out of love, love for one another, and ultimately, love for yourself.

If you have a limiting physical restriction, it would help you to ask yourself what the physical restriction is giving you that you may not otherwise have had. Has it caused you to spend more time with your parents than is usual? Has it assisted you to develop qualities such as persistence, courage or compassion?

What does the restriction represent to you? As you give yourself the answers to what it represents for you, you will begin to uncover the true reason for the illness and become aware of the family karma you have come to assist your family with. Whether you experience your condition as negative or positive, it is truly love in action. You can resolve these issues emotionally and spiritually by releasing all that restricts you. When a soul chooses this kind of experience, it does so with great care. Not only does a soul choose with great care, it also summons forth advisors and considers all possibilities before embarking consciously on such a journey. Not only does the soul choose a life with such physical restrictions in order to serve others, it does so primarily to serve its own growth. If there were no value in the experience, then the experience would not have been chosen. You are growth-seeking beings, and this is how choices are made.

If you have an inherited condition and are concerned that you may take it with you into your next life, then cease worrying. There is a law that says that you cannot leave something until you love it. Loving is about allowing and accepting. As you accept your physical restriction, you release it. On a deeper level, you will one day see all the beauty and love that this issue has brought you. As you come to the realisation that all has been in service to you and your family, you will bless the condition and thank it for its service to you. As you release something with love, you cease placing your attention on it; and as you cease placing your attention on it, it ceases to be in your experience. Good health to you!

What else is there to be learned from our biological family?

It is important for you to know that, although we speak of inherited thoughts and emotions, you are not constrained by them unwillingly. We have spoken about opposites, have we not? The family blueprint that you inherited was chosen by you because it provided you with opportunities to develop in the areas you had previously selected. Perhaps you wanted to develop the art of forgiveness, understanding, compassion, determination, courage, or any number of soul qualities.

Not all of your feelings actually originate with you. Many of you who are reading this material are the children of those who have experienced wars, and as with all wars, there is trauma. These traumas have become a part of your emotional make-up and have also dictated the way in which your own parents were able to do their parenting. As you step back and look at your family in the light of this information, you can clearly see how thoughts and feelings are passed down through a family. It is those very thoughts and feelings which 'one didn't talk about' that cause most emotional entanglements. These 'traumas' awaken a child to the pain of the parent. As it comes into the world a child seeks harmony. It is then the natural tendency of the child to alleviate some of the parent's pain by voluntarily carrying the emotional burden within its own body. It does so out of love for the parent.

Emotion is healed at the point when you can honour your parents for what they have delivered to you, for they truly have been in service to you, as you have been in service to them. All that they are became a part of you, and it has been your part in the family karma to evolve those aspects. When you understand that everything was pre-planned and by choice, you can then honour the gift that your parents have given you. At this point, you are released to the true essence of your soul. As you release your parents with love and honour, your soul will have more and more influence upon you, and your life will be filled with joy.

If you disown parents, you deny the choices you made prior to this lifetime. And you deny the essence of who you are, for you are, in part, their creation. You hold within you their characteristics, thoughts, ideas, and beliefs. You are dominated by them only if you believe that you are, for you are here to evolve the family, and in doing so, you evolve the family of humanity, for as one person releases all that is restrictive, the planet is changed forever.

Chapter 13

Good and Evil

Many religious philosophies teach that there is a battle between good and evil. Even many 'new age' thinkers are saying this. What is your view?

When you speak of evil, we understand you to mean that which is inherently bad or that which is inherently 'godless'. There is nothing that is inherently bad. Two emotional states exist in the Universe. One is love, the other fear. That which you call 'evil' came forth out of fear. Great fear causes separation, and at times that separation can cause a personality to split off into a state where it appears to be totally separate from its source, from God. However, this is illusion, for there is no one and nothing that exists beyond the love of God. All things exist within the mind and heart of God, even those that you may judge to be evil.

Let us appeal to your logic here. If God is 'All-That-Is', and all exists within God, how could there be a battle between good and evil? This would suggest that there are those who are not part of God, and that denies the very nature of God. If there truly were a battle between good and evil, then this would suggest that God is divided against himself, or the Goddess against herself. This is not so.

The Devil and other such entities are the creation of humanity, just as God is the creation of humanity. You see, just as God was created in **your** image, you have also created the Devil in **your** image. Both are archetypes of your species' capabilities. They represent your greatest dreams and your worst nightmares. For humans, by their nature, are capable of great miracles, compassion, and kindness, and likewise capable of great cruelty and atrocities. However, all this is merely a reflection of your inner state. When you are in a state of fear, you act in ways that reflect that fear. Fear separates; it does not unite. In many ways, your religious notion that God is above you and superior to you has contributed to the expression of fear, or 'evil' as you may call it.

We hear you when you say, "How could a person who is robbing or torturing another be afraid? Clearly they are bad or evil." And we say to you: What does the perpetrator need to believe in order to commit such an act? Would a joyful person do such a thing? Would someone who felt they had self-worth commit such acts? Or would a person who felt separated from his or her source, from God, be inclined to do such things? It is exactly so.

So many of you believe that something went wrong with life on Earth, that some error was made and humanity 'fell from grace' in some way. This view of the world has led you to need redemption and has caused you to place the responsibility for that redemption upon others. The Christ is a case in point. From one perspective, it is indeed the 'Christ' that will redeem you, but again, we speak not of the man Jesus, or of any individual soul or 'son' of God. We speak of that which is represented by the Christ. The Christ represents the unified heart, the heart that understands that it is connected to all life, and that all life, all things, all beings, are not only connected to itself, but are a part of itself. In this sense, yes, the Christ, or rather the realisation of the Christ as a level of consciousness, is indeed your redemption, because it is through this level of awareness that you will finally be able to see truth. The truth that you will see is that you have **never** been separate from the Source. No one is ever separate, and all that you perceive as separate is only separate because of the way you perceive it. There is no reality; there is only your perception of it.

> "The truth that you will see is that you have **never** been
> separate from the Source; no one is ever separate."

So how did this viewpoint come about? It came about because it was part of the challenge which you had decided to set yourselves. As a soul, you are a growth-seeking being, and as such, you seek growth in all that you do. The physical plane is one of the many playgrounds in which you play. You entered into the physical world in order that you may more completely understand your spiritual nature. It has been your greatest teacher and ally. As you entered the physical world, you began to associate very strongly with it. Your physical body had physical sensations. It could be hurt, indeed harmed and even killed. Therefore, your primary goal as you entered was survival of the physical organism. The physical body became 'all that is' for you. Without it, you ceased to exist. Despite your deep association with the physical, you still had your eternal connection to your Greater Self, to your Soul, to the Source of All Life. Your spiritual self had planted within you an atom, and this atom gently pulsates with the will to love. It acts like a magnet, drawing you towards self-realisation as God/Goddess, drawing you towards love.

With the experience of seeing the physical vessel as being who you are, coupled with your 'inner knowing' of who you truly are, you began to search for the inner knowing, to understand it. Just as you had associated yourself with that which was physical, that which was external, you then began externalising the 'inner knowing' into that which was external, and thus came the invention of a personalised God. In the same way the Devil and evil forces were born, for they represented your fears.

Having said this, we remind you that the Universe is a vast place, with souls that are at vastly different levels of evolution. There are indeed non-physical beings that are as fear-bound as many humans. However, as we have said before and will repeat many more times, you create your own reality. Therefore, you create each event in your life. In the Universe all is in vibration, and you draw things to you according to your vibration, for all like things are drawn to one another. Think of 'evil' forces and you will begin to vibrate with what you equate to be evil. As you do this, you begin to attract that 'evil' into your reality, and so indeed such energies can be yours. Think of love, it is yours; think of fear, it is yours; think of beauty, it is yours; think of ugliness, and it is yours. You are what you think you are. So how do you want to think of yourself today?

> "Think of love, it is yours;
> think of fear, it is yours."

There is nothing wrong with you, there has never been anything wrong with you, and there never will be anything wrong with you. You have free will, do you not? For free will to exist, there must be allowing. For allowing to exist, there must be acceptance. For acceptance to exist, there must be love. For love is the total and complete acceptance of what is. You are exquisitely loved. Every cell in your body, every hair on your head, every particle that makes up your being, all are held in absolute unconditional love at all times. It makes no difference what you have done in the past, are doing now, nor what you will do in the future, you are always loved. And why? Because love is the ultimate truth, it is the nature of 'God'; it is the nature of who you are. The key is for you to remember reasons to love yourself, for that is your salvation, to love yourself. For as you do this, you love others and you experience others as being an extension of yourself. It is with this realisation that peace washes over you and you remember who you truly are. You remember that you never left God, you remember that not only are you loved, you are love itself. You remember that you are God!

> "Because love is the ultimate truth,
> it is the nature of who you are."

This life and all the lives you have lived are a journey. It can be a joyous journey if you so choose. You are on this journey by your own choice; you are in the physical because you have chosen to be in the physical world, not for any other reason. There is no higher authority that has coerced you to be physical or who has sent you to the physical world. Part of your journey is to remember that you are the creator and that you are in charge; it is not any other way.

There are so many of you that lament the physical, yearning to be elsewhere and perhaps working hard on spiritual matters, for that promises to be a ticket out of your physical 'misery'. Let us share this with you: You cannot leave anything until you love it. And why do we say this? Are we being harsh, telling you to put up with where you are, or telling you that you have to obey and get things right before you can leave the planet? No! We are telling you this because it is Universal Law. Let us explain.

When you love something, you accept it. When you accept something, you cease resisting it; when you no longer resist something, you cease being focused on it. This is the key. When you love anything, you release it, and you become free. If you lament being in the physical, see it as a trap, or as a punishment, or as a place where you need to be in order to become good enough, then you are resisting it. When you resist it, you are focused on it; when you focus on it, it is yours! It cannot be any other way. When you focus on something, it increases, gets bigger, and you end up with more of it. Therefore, the only way to move out of the physical world and into the non-physical is to do exactly what you set out to do in the first place, that is to love it. Indeed, yes, to love it. To love every aspect of Earth life. To love its peoples, to love the rocks, the trees, the stones, the cities, the mountains, the deserts, the animals, and the plants. To celebrate her oceans and to honour the beauty, creativity, and delight of your fellow human beings. Love is the key to your release. Love is your salvation. When you reach this exquisite and delicious place, you will not want to leave. You will say: "My, my, this is the most delicious, exciting, wonderful place I have ever been in." There is nothing more wonderful than being physically present and consciously in union with the Source of all life. This is why so many of you are in the physical, this is why so many of you return time and time again, and why so many of you came to this place. It is a wonderful place to be!

How can we understand violent crime? We often hear of crimes involving violence that seem to be totally senseless.

Violence is always a reaction to fear. The ones who are committing the violent acts have a perception of danger. They perceive that their victims are a threat to their own security, and therefore they act in accordance with their perception. In the perception of those who act in a threatening way, a loss of freedom is their greatest threat. Therefore, those who pose a threat to that freedom are seen to present the greatest danger.

So what are the causes of such behaviours? It is a complex matter, and we will explain it to you in the simplest way we know how. First, ask yourself the question: What does the assailant need to believe about himself and the world in order to choose to act in such a way? Again, we know, just as you know, that one who is experiencing self as the physical extension of God will not act in these ways. Those who believe that abundance, love, health and well-being, and the ability to create are part of their very nature will not act in this way. It is *always* limiting beliefs that lead anyone to act in ways that harm others. Ultimately, they harm themselves. For as your culture seeks to 'correct' them, they further take on the belief that they are not worthy, which in turn leads to deeper feelings of powerlessness. It is those who feel powerless that behave in such ways. They seek to overpower you for they are seeking what they are missing, and that is authentic power. Authentic power comes from knowing that you are connected to the Source of all life. Authentic power comes from knowing that you have the power to create what you want. Authentic power comes from knowing that you are not only loved by God, but that you are, in essence, one and the same thing; you are God. *as me.*

> "Authentic power comes from knowing that you are connected
> to the Source of all life."

There are those in your culture who are what we call the disowned ones. They have largely been disowned as they emerged into your physical world and have not had the opportunity to form any bonds of love with one or both parents, usually with neither parent. Even though you may not have what you term a 'good' relationship with your parents, you still have love for them, and they for you. A disowned child, perhaps one who was not planned, not wanted, or was raised by those who lacked the emotional skills or even an interest in raising a child, will not have bonded with any individual. Although some of you may have been rejected by your own parents, in most cases there are other adults with whom you will bond. When a child does not bond with anyone at all, it lacks the knowledge of love. It also lacks the knowledge of pain. Without bonding, a child cannot feel emotions, cannot interpret emotions, and simply does not know what either love or pain is. Therefore, when adult, this individual may express themselves in very violent ways or ways that you may consider cruel or 'evil'.

Such a soul is one that has had many lifetimes of feeling rejected and the only solution to this is to offer unconditional love. Part of that love, as you teach them how to feel, will be to teach the individual that they are responsible for their actions. Teaching them how to feel is the key. This individual has experienced, and indeed experiences, so much emotional pain that they have separated themselves from it. This is similar to the way that personalities can split off and cause mental disorders. Part of your response as a loving, healing human being is to teach all those who share your world with you what feelings are, and how feelings teach you what is appropriate and inappropriate. Your violent criminals are indeed worthy of your greatest compassion and your greatest acceptance, for this is what they yearn for. They do not deserve your scorn or punishment; however, this does not deny them the responsibility that must be taken for all actions.

The solution to all your problems of crime and violence is to make a shift in the way you view yourselves. You educate your young in accordance with the way you view yourselves. If you believe that you need to do and be and say things in order to be worthy, you will educate your children in like manner. This self-view extends the thought and the idea that you are 'less than'. In a culture where conformity is emphasized over natural tendency and talent, a child will tend to rebel. Rebellion is always caused by pain. That pain causes resistance, and resistance can lead to behaviour that is threatening. Self-appreciation is the solution to all your woes. As you appreciate yourself, you begin to love yourself; as you love yourself, you love and appreciate others; as you do so, you begin to allow others to be who they are because you are allowing yourself to be who you are. If all of you would only allow yourselves to be who you are, you would have world peace in the twinkling of an eye. You do not need to work hard to improve matters; you simply need to stop resisting and pushing against all that is true. The truth is that you are loved beyond all measure.

There is talk about secret governments, conspiracies, and even aliens who are out to control us. What is your perspective on this?

Let us restate the two ultimate truths. First truth: You are exquisitely loved without condition. Second Truth: You create your own reality. Not some of it, not most of it, but all of it. All that we offer in this book is a reiteration of those truths.

All humans are at differing levels of evolution and development. Many of you have had many hundreds of lifetime experiences, and many more now on Earth have had fewer lives and less experience. One of the phases of life on Earth is to become acquainted with power: the experiencing of personal power, the wielding of it, being subject to it, all aspects of power. Conspiracies and 'forces' that work against you are the product of those who have forgotten that all the power lies within them.

Yes, we hear you say, "But there is evidence that 'they' are doing this or that 'they' are doing that." And we say to you: To whom are they doing it? Are they doing it to you? Is that what you want in your reality? We are not saying you should bury your head in the sand and stand by idly if a company puts chemical waste into a nearby river, not at all. But we remind you of this: what kind of world do you want?

This planet is at a normal stage of evolution. As we look at your galaxy and all of the inhabited planets that we are acquainted with, Earth is doing rather well. To put things in your terms, there are planets that are much 'worse' than yours, just as there are planets that are much 'better' than yours. For you to understand this, you must understand the phases of soul evolution. Your consensus reality is a reflection of your consensus of beliefs. You believe that the Universe is a hostile place and that you must protect yourself against it. This is typical of souls who have not yet awakened to the essence of who they are. The belief that 'if only they wouldn't do that, then I could be this' is fairly typical of mature souls that have a glimpse of their greater selves but are still struggling with all the fears and power struggles of where they have been in the past.

What this is all about is your reluctance to acknowledge who you are. Someone, somewhere, convinced you that you were worthless, powerless beings, and now you are busy convincing yourselves of it, too. Cease that! You create your own reality. What kind of world do you want? Are you ready to acknowledge your own power? Are you ready to acknowledge the power of love? Do you have the courage to succeed? For that is what it will take. The entire world is saying that you are weak and defenceless. Are you willing to be the lone voice that speaks up and says, "I am one with God, and my greatest and deepest desire is to love?"

Chapter 14

True Inner Guidance

How can we know the difference between true inner guidance and wishful thinking?

Shall we throw the cat amongst the pigeons and tell you that there is no difference! What we hear you asking is this: "When I get an idea to do something, how do I know it is the right thing to do?" Perhaps this is based on your past experiences of things not turning out the way you expected them to. Let us first deal with that subject.

When things don't turn out the way you want them to, so many of you have become accustomed to telling yourself that 'it was never meant to be', or you say 'the Universe has other plans for me'. We are not talking of things that are unimportant to you, but of things that you have truly wanted and have not come to fruition. As we have said before, your feelings are your best friends, and in this way, wishful thinking and inner guidance are one and the same. For when you think of what you want and begin to align with your inner sense of joy at the idea of having, or doing, or being that thing, your Inner Self begins immediately to bring that thing to you. You receive inspiration, and you are encouraged with good and positive feelings that energise you.

In your day-to-day life you have decisions to make concerning business, or what road to take on your journey home. Tuning into your feelings is the best way to practice sensing and acting upon inner guidance. Through daily 'checking in' to your feelings, you will gradually become so aware of your inner guidance that you will sense subtle changes concerning seemingly unimportant things. You see, your soul wishes you a life of joy, love, abundance, good health, and happiness, and it seeks to steer you in those directions through all of your waking hours. The litmus test for deciding if what you are thinking is 'wishful thinking' or inner guidance is to sense your feelings. If you cannot sense your feelings, or define them, then sense your breathing. Your breathing, the physical manifestation of the drinking in of life force energy, is reactive to your emotions, even very subtle ones.

Sit quietly and think of a decision you want to make, even a seemingly unimportant choice between two holiday destinations. Imagine yourself, let's say, in Greece, and then imagine yourself in Spain. What happens to your breathing? No difference between the two? If that is the case, define what you are looking for and how you would like to enjoy your holiday time. Your Greater Self already knows the opportunities and conditions in both places. Once you have defined what it is you want, imagine yourself again in both places. The picture that summons the more expanded, easier, fuller breaths is the place to go, for your soul is telling you that that place is more perfectly in line with what you want. For those of you who have difficulty in knowing what you are feeling, observation of your breathing is an excellent place to start. If this exercise is too subtle for you, visualise those things that are less related to one another. For example, imagine doing something that you don't like doing, and watch your breathing. Then imagine doing something that you love to do, and feel the difference! This is your own built-in Yes/No mechanism!

Wishful thinking is what we encourage. Stretch your imagination, visualise all the possibilities and do not limit yourself. You can have what you want, and your Greater Self wants you to have it!

You said to just do what feels good to us. Taking drugs feel good, so should we ignore the consequences?

When we speak of 'feeling good', we do not speak of the momentary elevated feelings of excitement that a person may feel when stealing a handbag, or doing any other things that stimulate chemical reactions in the body. This kind of 'feeling good' is temporary, as are the effects of drugs. Those who are addicted to drugs, or those who are engaged in other kinds of addictive behaviours, are not coming from a place of joy; they are coming from a place of lack. All addictions serve to try to fill a place that feels empty within that individual. Humans wrestle with two basic limiting beliefs: "I am powerless" and "I am not loved". Drugs and behaviours that heighten the senses seek to deaden the inner feelings of loneliness and despair that many humans feel.

When we say, "Do what feels good", we are talking about joyous adventure. When you embark upon joyous adventure, your heart is open and you are like a child, ready to embrace new possibilities in all that you encounter. Drug taking, for the most part, seeks to deaden negative feelings, and therefore is an action that springs forth from lack, not from joy. When you pursue that which makes you feel good, you are more open to the flow of creative energies. You feel enlivened, inventive, and enthusiastic about life, your future, and the people around you. Again, we repeat, do what feels good, for it is good for you!

How can people who have learned to struggle for things in life, turn that energy around and experience more joy without feeling that they are slacking off?

We see that the majority of you have inherited the belief that you must work hard for all that you have. This stems from your inner feeling of worthiness or lack thereof.

So many of you have such strong beliefs about worthiness, and although you are beginning to understand that each individual creates his or her own reality, you still hold onto strong judgements concerning worthiness. The Universe is totally impartial. It cares not whether you are a just person or an unjust person, and it cares not whether you are a hard-working person or a lazy person. The only thing the Universe responds to is your attention to a particular subject. If you feel that you must work hard in order to win other people's approval, then that will be your experience. If two people were to win the lottery, one who was a grumpy man who never smiled, was always impolite and troublesome with his neighbours, and only cared about making money and lots of it—and he actually won a considerable sum—and the other was a hard-working single mother who hadn't taken a holiday for several years, who viewed life as a struggle—and she only won the smallest prize, you would all scream, "That isn't fair!" despite the fact that this is consistent with Universal law.

The Universe is impartial. You are creators; you create your own reality. Your reality is your choice. Your reality is your choice. Your reality is your choice! You don't create some of it, you don't create most of it, you create all of it. You choose your reality inasmuch as you choose to think the thoughts you are thinking and to feel the feelings you are feeling. You are beings of free will. Free will does not come in measured doses. You either have it, or you do not. So which is it to be?

If you, like many others, have been taught that it is noble to struggle, then cease doing so immediately. Ask yourself this question: What is the pay-off to living with struggle? So many of you belong to unspoken and unnamed clubs. Let us name them for you. There is the "Struggle and Debt Club", the "Difficult Husband Club", the "Nagging Wife Club", the "My Parents Don't Love Me Club", the "I Am Wounded and Abandoned Club", the "My Body Is Sick and Weak Club". All these unspoken clubs, which many of you belong to, have a pay-off. You have developed a culture whereby you identify with others who have similar wounds and difficulties. These become your confidantes and your allies. Although there can be great value in this sort of comradeship, for there is much to learn from a mirror when it presents itself to you, what many of you fear is the loss of recognition, sympathy, love, and compassion when you finally rescind your membership of one of these clubs.

If you are struggling with a physical, emotional, or financial condition in your life, ask yourself this: What is the pay-off for me? What am I getting out of this? What decisions about my life would I need to make if this problem suddenly went away? Are my relationships based on being supported with this problem?

So many of you hold onto the very problem that you seek to rid yourself of because you fear the consequences of releasing it. Also, if a worldview, or an illness, or a financial condition has been in your experience for so long that it has literally become a part of you, it is interwoven in your energy. Then the fear arises that, if you release it, who are you? Once a condition becomes concretised in this way, becoming a part of you, it takes consistent choice on your part to create the new condition and belief you want to have. If there is something that you want that you do not already have, then you have not wanted it enough. All conditions exist because you allow them to. Are you ready to release struggle along with the belief that you are only deserving if there is struggle and hard work? Be honest with your answer and you will know instantly how to resolve the situation.

How do we stay centred when loved ones around us are experiencing pain and suffering?

You are creator, are you not? And is not the person who suffers pain also creator? As you acknowledge yourself and the other as creators of your experience, you as the observer of that suffering, and the other as the attractor of that suffering, then you will both be empowered. You see, pain and suffering are the way in which others call out to you for love.

Remember that it is your beliefs and thoughts that create circumstances. As you stand back and observe the suffering of another, ask yourself what this person needs to have believed about themselves in order to have attracted such circumstances? As you ask this, the answer will come, for you will have moved from pity, which incapacitates the one pitied, into compassion which empowers those who are challenged.

If you have a question, the answer is always love. When you understand that the other is making a request for love, you then have the opportunity to move into your own centre of love. At this point you become powerful and centred. Because you are sure of your own ability to create your experience, for you have chosen to move into love and compassion in the midst of suffering, you pass on that message to those who are suffering.

You see, suffering is relative. Let us relate a story of a young man. This young man had been tormented all of his life with deep feelings of grief that he could not express. When he was a young child his father died, and his mother remarried just months afterwards. She remarried a total of four times before he was 20, and it seemed to him that every year or two he had a new father, one who would leave, and then his mother would begin again with courting and dating. This left him angry, but above all in pain.

He never had much success in dating young women. All of them complained that he had no feelings, and they left him. He got to a stage in his life where he wanted to change, but did not know how. Therapy did not work for him because he had experienced violence at the hands of one or two of the surrogate fathers and so he had taught himself to be 'strong' and not to cry. His early childhood decision was not to feel. As he grew older he got more desperate, unable to express feelings, and also unable to find and keep a companion. Just as he was at the end of his tether, he had a serious motorbike accident that caused him to break both arms and both legs. He spent the next six weeks on his back, helpless in a hospital. No longer could he run away from his feelings into work, alcohol, or racing his bike. He had to face himself. Those who did not know him thought it was a tragedy. Those who knew him thought it was the best thing that could have happened.

When you observe suffering, we encourage you to remember not only that it is a call for love that is being made, but also ask to yourself how the suffering is serving that individual. If it were not serving that individual, it would not be in his or her life. As personalities and as souls, you only hold onto what works for you, and that includes suffering.

One of my spiritual goals is to embrace all that I can with unconditional love. How can I accept someone who behaves in ways that are offensive to me?

We delight at this question! Do you know that you are creator? That you are the attractor of all conditions into your life? As you determine something to be 'offensive', you are in the mode of resisting it, pushing against it. As you push against it, it launches itself into your experience, for that is where your attention is.

The Universe responds to attention. As you set the intention to embrace all with unconditional love, then your attention to that subject brings to the forefront all that is associated with it. The opposite of unconditional is conditional, is it not? So, as you set forth to create unconditional, the Universe makes clear to you all of the conditions you have in place that are blocking your experience of unconditional love, and this includes human behaviours you disapprove of.

If you were to set the intention of becoming more patient, everything to do with patience would then bubble up to the surface for you to release. What this means is that all that generally makes you impatient will be presented to you so that you may take the opportunity to release it forever. Have you not heard the saying? "Be careful what you ask for, for you may get it." It brings a smile to us when we hear such questions, for we are then able to prove to you that you are indeed creator. That which you love glides into your reality and that which you judge marches in right along side it. Just as we have explained that each subject is actually two subjects, the positive aspect and the negative aspect, the same applies to all that you desire. If you want peace, you will need to release turmoil and anger. If you want abundance, thoughts of poverty will need to be transformed.

When the Master said, "Love your enemies," he was referring to this process, for those whom you judge, hate, or condemn have come to show you yourself. They are your teachers!

Having said all of this, we tell you it is your right to determine your own boundaries and what is permissible in your own home. However, we advise you to remember that no one is in your life by accident; all is by design.

Chapter 15

Religion

―――――――――

What is the role of religion and why did we create it?

To understand the role of religion, you must view humanity as a group entity that is evolving through many stages. You can liken these stages to the stages of life that you experience in one lifetime. For example, we refer to infant, baby, young, mature, and old souls. You chose as souls to enter into this system of things in order to experience comparison, opposites. In truth, the statement of who you are, is: "I am God/Goddess, and I have dominion over myself." The experience of religion gave you for the most part: "I am God and I have dominion over you." In this scenario you became subservient to an externalised image of God and ceased to experience the inner God and the knowing that all true authority comes from within.

The experience of physicality created a scenario where you began to see all things as external, and so it was with God. As you began to get increasingly involved in physical life, all that was physical became more real. Your physical body had senses; it could feel in ways you had never felt before. As a newly arrived soul, you were often in survival mode, living by just scraping by, hunting or begging for food, living from one meal to the next. As you had the experience of physical hunger, and felt the pangs of hunger, your hunger and your physicality are what became real. In this stage of development on the physical plane, your true source, which is spiritual, became less and less important because what was 'real' for you was physical. You experienced 'real' hunger, 'real' pain, and 'real' sexual drive. Physicality became real. In its realness, the elements and other physical entities became real sources of pain, fear, and discomfort, and so you entered into a mode of defensiveness.

It was then that the need for religion came about. As you are beings of comparison, your gods began to take the form of archetypes of the ideals you strove for. The gods were on the opposite side of the axis, as it were. You invented gods that were warlike heroes, gods that you could call upon to help you in battle or save you from wild animals or from tribes that were competing for the same land and resources. Your perception of yourselves as vulnerable beings, living in a dangerous physical world where the end of physical life was a very 'real' threat, led you to create gods that were an archetype of the 'ideal'. They were strong.

In this way, archetypes were created for purity, grace, compassion, love, wisdom, and justice—all qualities that you strove for. As identification with the physical became stronger and stronger, so the gods became more powerful and more 'superhuman'. Religions served the purpose of assisting you to focus on your true divine qualities. It is not that God gave you religion. It is humanity that provided religion for itself, because each of you has a deep knowing of your destiny. Irrespective of whether or not you are aware of your eternal self and your real reason for being physically present, your psyche is aware of the greater picture, and it is in this way that the human psyche provides itself with tools to assist in its own growth. Yes, you are both student and teacher in your own world. You decide what to learn and how to learn it, and you implement it. You are in charge.

Religion ceases to play any major role once a soul begins to remember the essence of who it is. At this stage, the personality in question begins to see itself as part of a greater picture, as a part of 'God', and begins to see itself as directly relating to this 'god' as a force, thereby depersonalising it in the process of recognising the power that resides within it. This is the process of maturation; it is where the individual soul begins to get a taste of what was meant when the Nazarene stated, "I and the Father are one." For indeed, this one had realised that the creative force of the Universe, 'God', resided within. This is the process of blending. It is for this very purpose that you incarnated on Earth in the first place.

The maturation process takes many, many lifetimes. The majority of you take somewhere between 200 and 300 lifetimes to complete this process. You will pass through all the different stages, and religion will play different roles in your many lifetimes. As part of this evolution, you will have several lifetimes where religion will play the central role in your life. This central role will lead you into experiences of priesthood and service; this is a necessary part of your development. The priestly role (Priest, Rabbi, Shaman, Nun, Monk, etc.) will further awaken in you the need to realise 'God' whilst physically present, for this is your objective. Although on the face of it, it would seem that the doctrines of many religions go against what we are offering here, it is beneficial to bear in mind that it is the 'role' that is important to development, not the individual beliefs.

Who was Jesus Christ, and why does he seem to be so important?

First, let us make clear that Jesus and the Christ are not one and the same thing, but that 'Christ' is indeed a consciousness that was embodied by a man called Jesus. Jesus the Nazarene was an ordinary human being just like yourself, if any of you could be called ordinary!

Jesus was an old soul; he had had many, many lifetimes and was also the Moses of old. His purpose for being present at the time was to anchor on the Earth plane the consciousness of unity through love, acceptance, and allowing. It is for this reason that he is so strongly associated with forgiveness, for the main thrust of his teaching was the teaching of love.

The religious tradition of the Jewish people had been very rules-based. It accurately reflected the stage of development that humanity had reached at that time. However, as humanity has evolved, a teacher has always come along to assist with the next stage. This is what Jesus did. From this perspective, it is not possible to talk about Jesus without talking about Gautama, the Buddha. For these two great sons of God came forth fairly close to one another in order to help humanity move forward.

The era that followed these teachers was dominated by fear, violence, pestilence and war. It was a dark period. However, it was a necessary step to go through. This period of history was about humans discovering power, how to use it and how to come to terms with it. Teachings of the Christ and the Buddha, although not adhered to, were necessary at the time for the purpose of holding up an ideal. Without the presence of this energy, the 'Dark Ages' would have been significantly darker.

What the Christ did was to implant the ideal of love through the heart. Jesus the Nazarene became fully blended with his essence self whilst in physical form. This made way for him to allow the Christ (love) aspect of God to enter into him. This, in essence, was allowing 'God to walk among men'.

Gautama, who became Buddha, was also fully blended with his essence, which allowed the Buddhaic (wisdom) aspect of 'God to walk among men' in the same way. As you look at history, and particularly at the past 100 years, you can see how the energies that these two great beings have brought to the planet are now coming to fruition. As a species, your desire for unity is growing and your capacity for compassion and allowing is growing alongside it.

When Jesus spoke of the return of the Christ, he was not speaking of the personal return of Jesus the Nazarene, but he was speaking as the Christ, of the Christ. This return is occurring, and will continue to unfold in two ways. First, the return of the Christ is a mass event, meaning that the principle of love is awakening within many who are now beginning to sense and feel their essence or soul. This event in itself is responsible for the upswing in interest in spiritual matters and in self-examination. More and more people are awakening to the experience and to the idea that they are more than just their physical selves. There is a deeper understanding of who they are and what their purpose is. This grand awakening of humanity is also preparing you for the next great teacher. Just as John the Baptist was said to prepare the way for the Christ, you who are awakening are preparing the way for the teachers to come. What awaits you is more than one teacher, and these teachers will solidify that which has been called 'new age' thinking.

The greatest change that will come about is the shift in your perception to acknowledge that you create your own reality. Vast changes will occur in the fields of medicine, education, and even government. Your relationship to the animal and plant kingdoms will also change. In part, the dolphins will assist you with this by imparting their knowledge; however, most of the changes will be led by humanity.

Chapter 16

Physical Death and Disease

Why do we experience physical death and disease?

We could say that fear causes death and disease. That, expressed in the simplest way, is the truth from our perspective. You are the physical extension of a non-physical entity; you are a finger of God protruding into the physical world. As such, you are tapped into, and are part of, the same creative force that created the Universe that you know. It is this energy that flows through you that not only creates your physical body, but also sustains it in much the same way that food and water sustains your physical body.

> *"You are a finger of God protruding*
> *into the physical world."*

It is this very same energy that you mould with your thoughts in order to bring what you are thinking of into your experience. There are but two real emotions that you can feel; one is love, the other is fear. We have already stated that the primary law of the Universe is Love. This Law of Love is about the complete and total acceptance of what is; it is about allowing; it is expansive; it does not restrict in any way. When you are in the mode of allowing and accepting, you are fully open to the creative forces of the Universe. This means that your body is fully nourished and does not age. Have you not noticed how joyful people seem to look physically younger? And those who focus on the negative are often sick and poorly? This is no coincidence. It is joy that leads to eternal life. When we speak of eternal life, we speak of life in an ageless physical body, for you already have eternal life. Part of mastering the Earth plane is making conscious choices on how and when to depart physicality. Not all of you will do this, but many of you will. Many souls will simply choose to have many lifetimes on the physical plane and then go on to other planes of existence once the physical shell has been discarded. However, for many, the challenge is to remain in the physical, lifetime after lifetime, until a state of fearlessness is achieved. This state of being fearless, or to state it positively, the state of love and of allowing, is exquisite, and it is what many of you have been calling enlightenment.

> *"When you are in the mode of allowing and accepting,*
> *you are fully open to the creative forces of the Universe."*

Your identification with the physical world has caused death and disease. Although on one level we can say that physical death is 'unnatural', it was also known beforehand that this would be one of the 'side effects' of consciousness entering into physicality. Death is part of the Earth experience, but that can and will change in your future. Not only will death change, but there have also always been a few who have mastered physical existence to the extent that they have often lived in a youthful state for between 300 and 500 years. Many of these 'enlightened ones' have lived in India and the Himalayas, but each region of the planet has known such men and women. When this change comes about depends largely on humanity.

You have already seen how you are getting to be older, living longer lives in the past few generations, have you not? Living longer has come about because there has been a shift in consciousness; it has nothing to do with nutrition. Many of your young ones are living on so-called 'junk foods', yet they are maturing earlier and getting taller and taller. In recent decades, your focus has shifted away from 'survival' and many of you are planning your lives, instead of just allowing life to happen to you. The economic shift has taken much fear out of your lives, although other points of stress have entered. However, on the whole, your lives are now freer from fear. You have so many more choices open to you, many more forms of work and pleasure, and you are beginning to sense and experience that you are creators.

As time progresses over the next 30 years or so, more work will take place from the home, and more of you will be working for yourselves instead of for corporations. This will allow many more of you to tap into your desires and passions, expressing yourselves more freely. This freedom to create will lead to more joy, more abundance, and hence to longer and longer lives.

On the whole the biggest breakthrough that will come for you will be the mass shift in perception towards acknowledging that you are creators of your own reality. We have already spoken of shifts in spiritual perception following the upcoming 'contact' with the dolphins; however, all these changes will be underpinned by your acceptance of yourselves as creators. This will take your species out of survival mode. The majority of human beings are in survival mode; they live from day to day, wondering where the next meal is coming from. In your industrialized nations, you live from month to month, often becoming a slave to your possessions, working long hours to make house, car and other payments. This will begin to dissolve as more of you choose to do what you love to do. As you tap into doing what you love to do, you automatically become more open to the flow of universal creative energy. This openness to the flow creates radiant health, and it creates more opportunities to create even more. You naturally become more abundant.

At the moment, the 'wealthy' nations are becoming 'sicker', not because wealth is bad, but because you are creating from a position of lack. You do not believe that there is sufficient to go around and hold on to the belief that you must work hard for wealth or must 'deserve' it in some way. Much of this behaviour has come from religious imprinting, but essentially it all comes out of your feelings of separation from God, from your source.

During the Cold War, many of you put out a call from your hearts. Religion had 'failed' you and science was no longer providing answers. You were asking who you were and what was the meaning of your existence. It has been this great call that has brought about these changes. In essence, you called upon God, not the God of your forefathers, but your true one and only God, your Inner Self, the All-That-Is that lives within you, your Soul. Your Soul has responded to this call and has been active in your life, inspiring you, encouraging you.

Your physical body is but a temporary vessel and it responds directly to your thoughts. Your thoughts precede emotion, and emotion is energy in motion. As you look at the world from the point of view of 'survival', whether that is on the African savannah or in the concrete jungle of your contemporary cities, your body responds with tightness, vigilance, and chemicals that eventually tire the body. Could you imagine being 'alert' and 'awake' 24 hours a day for 40 years or so, always on the lookout for impending disaster or for danger and foes? This is how most of you live! The majority of you are not even aware of this; the fear and vigilance have become such a natural part of your day-to-day living that you accept the tension and your body's shallow breathing as normal. You are not even aware that you are afraid.

You may even say, "I am not afraid of anything." Perhaps you do not fear being robbed or raped, but do you fear expressing your deepest feelings? Do you share your dreams and passion with those you love? Do you readily display your Inner Self, or do you keep things hidden for fear of being judged? Fear has become the disease of humans and you have accepted it as normal.

Part of the current transformation is because many of you are being confronted with your inner self, with all the feelings, wishes, dreams and desires that you have locked up inside. You are beginning to examine the monotony of your work, perhaps even your life. These questions are not going unanswered. It may seem to many of you as if you are currently experiencing crises, not knowing who you are or what you want, or perhaps being overwhelmed by emotions. However, for many of you this is occurring as you reach ever deeper within to find your true source. Earth life was supposed to be joyful, not a struggle! It will mean re-examining many of your beliefs and values.

For you to understand death and disease, it is important for us to reiterate that you create your own reality. Not some of it, not most of it, but all of it. And whilst we will encourage you to move into old age gracefully and to be in acceptance of it, it is not a 'necessary' experience, but an experience that has become part of the mass consciousness of your belief system. The belief system is that which you know as Earth.

> *"You create your own reality. Not some of it, not most of it,*
> *but all of it."*

Energy is moulded and formed by thought. Thought is the sculptor, the painter of your reality. Each cell in your body responds to your thoughts. See yourself as being frail and weak, and your body will respond by being frail and weak. The human body is fed by universal energy and that universal energy not only sustains the body, but also creates and re-creates the body. You are who you believe yourself to be, and universal energy will create within your experience an image that fits your beliefs.

There are many people who appear to be living joyful lives and yet they get sick and die. How does that fit in with what you are saying?

Not only do you have your own individual patterns, fears, and beliefs, but you also have mass beliefs that are generally accepted unquestioningly. It has been the challenging and changing of mass beliefs and consciousness that has been the 'cause' of many of your wars and natural disasters. Each of these events has created a change in direction for humanity or for the culture that created them.

Physical death has become a 'fact of life' for you. As you grew up, you watched your parents grow old and perhaps a grandparent die. Death, although a taboo subject in many cultures, has been a part of your life since early childhood. This means that it has become an undeniable fact in your mind. However, 'facts' are merely beliefs that have manifested over a long period of time. You create your own reality, and physical death is one of the 'facts' that your species has created in its reality. Even as you read these words, many of you are saying, "I can't believe this," or, "Well, the rest of the book makes sense... but this?" or, "It would be really nice, but I don't think it is possible." This is the power of mass beliefs.

Just as we have said that religious belief has more to do with geography than with fact, so it is with physical death. It has everything to do with belief, and nothing to do with the biological possibilities. As you believe in death, so it is, it is yours. So many of you, as you begin to get older, begin to anticipate the aging process and warn yourself in advance about all the things you won't be able to do or enjoy as you get older. As the first grey hair appears, you settle into getting old and accept a weakening body as a fact of life.

Death came about because of fear; it did not come about because the biological organism you are housed in is weak. As the fears grew, the more constricted the flow of universal energy became. The less energy you received, the more you grew weak and "old". As this condition progressed over many, many generations, the more it became accepted as the norm. As that happened, even the more joyful and fearless among you succumbed to the effects of illness, disease, and old age, for it had become a "fact of life".

How can we slow down or even reverse the aging process?

By uncovering what causes you fear and discarding it. Most human beings have at their core two powerful beliefs: "I am powerless" and "I am not loved". Even your greatest teachers, artists and heroes carry these two beliefs deep at their core; they are common to your entire species. It is by feeling these feelings, and not only them but also all the 'satellite' feelings that surround them, that you can free yourself from their grip. For as you feel and experience them, you begin to realise that they are just beliefs, they are not truth, and they begin to lose their power over you. For most of you, this is a lifetime job, for there is much in your world that appears to confirm that you are indeed powerless and indeed unloved.

Daily meditation, quiet time, a time for you and for contemplation, is essential on anyone's path of spiritual unfolding. You can read all the books you want and attend all the seminars you want, but if you do not value yourself enough to spend time just with yourself, your progress will be limited and often slow. It is during this quiet time that your inner self has the opportunity to communicate with you. This may be through thoughts that come into your head or through feelings, or inspiration, or just through a deeper sense of peace and tranquillity. The more accustomed you become to this alone time, the easier it becomes and the more will come forth from your inner self.

> "It is during this quiet time that your inner self has the opportunity
> to communicate with you."

This quiet time is also a time to feel, to feel anything that is there to be felt, be it sadness, loneliness, anger, rage, joy, delight, or inspiration. All feelings are valid, and what lies beneath all of your feelings are the impulses of your soul; what lies beneath all of this, is truth. It is in this truth that you are able to tap into the God/Goddess within. With this connection, you automatically become less fearful and therefore more relaxed. Discovering and living your life's purpose is the first step to longevity, and you do this by listening to your Inner Self.

What about abortion? Do you consider that to be murder or wrong?

The most direct answer that we can give is that abortion is not 'wrong', and it is not 'right' either. However, like all things, there are multiple levels and therefore more than one answer to the same question. In part, this explains why some spiritual sources of information seem to differ from one another. Each answer is given according to the level of the question.

Let us begin by making statements of absolute truth. First, you are the physical extension of a non-physical being. Second, you have absolute and total free will. Third, you create your own reality—not some of it, not most of it, but all of it. Therefore, the act of purposeful abortion is not only the creation of the mother, but also the creation of the incoming soul. In order to answer this question fully, we must look at it from both perspectives and from different levels.

Each of you draws experience to yourself through the attention that you have been giving to the subject. Some of your creations arise through deliberate attention, but most do not. At this point most of your creations result from attention to a subject or a thought that is not deliberate, not conscious. We say this for we know that you do not say to yourself, "I wish to get pregnant and then abort the child." The reasons for unwanted or unplanned pregnancies are as numerous and varied as there are women who create this experience. For example, there was a woman who had grown tired of her relationship with her husband. She no longer had romantic feelings and felt stuck in old ways and patterns. She met another man, fell in love, but continued to remain with her husband. As a result of her additional relationship, a pregnancy materialised. This pregnancy gave her the opportunity to make a very clear decision about what she wanted, the type of relationship she wanted, and with whom. The soul of the unborn infant was a soul that was very close to her, but not in the physical. This soul agreed, together with the soul of the woman, to create the experience as a service to her higher good. Indeed, there are simpler and easier ways to make this kind of decision, but as she had had a long history of repeating the same pattern in her relationships, the soul of the unborn foetus came to her aid, with her agreement on a subconscious level. In the end, she made a clear choice to terminate the pregnancy and was supported by her new relationship.

Many other women in this position have a quite different story. In your history pregnancy has been a symbol of shame, and many a young woman has been spirited away from family and friends to a secret location so as to hide the shame of a premarital relationship. This is still true for many of you today, although on a subconscious level. Many, many of you, although participating in sexual relationships outside the rules that governed the lives of your mothers and grandmothers, still carry much guilt about the joy of such physical relationships. Therefore, the old symbol of a young woman's shame becomes manifest as a result of your own guilty feelings. Therefore, you are faced with making a life-or-death choice, and then transfer all your guilt to the act of 'murder' instead of dealing with the much, much deeper issues at the heart of the matter. For others, the unplanned pregnancy can be about assisting the mate involved to make a commitment.

There are numerous reasons why such pregnancies are created and we could speak to you for many hours on the subject, giving you one example after the other. However, even were we to do so, our answer would be incomplete if we do not include the many reasons why the incoming infant would create this scenario.

As given in our first example, you can clearly see that some souls co-create a pregnancy that they know in advance will be terminated, simply to assist the 'mother' with a process. However, there are many different levels of souls. Some souls are more 'mature', more 'developed' than others, depending on their depth of Earth experience, which is largely, but not solely, determined by the number of incarnations they have experienced.

Each of you is multidimensional in nature. Although at one level, you understand fully that you are an eternal being, a powerful being, a blessed child of the divine, you have other levels with very strong beliefs concerning Earth life. Some souls are very impatient to return to the Earth, and make unwise choices regarding the host parents. An aborted child *could* be such a soul, one that has not looked carefully at the true situation but simply sees the opportunity to create a body for itself. However, it is not true that the 'child' can create a pregnancy without the mother's implicit permission, for all things are a co-creation. In such a case, there is a vibrational match between the thoughts of the 'child' and the thoughts of the 'mother'. It could be that the 'mother' has always feared having an unwanted pregnancy and worried about it incessantly each time she engaged in mating. This attention to the subject, if combined with sufficient emotion (fear), can draw such a circumstance to her. In this case, the 'baby' and the 'mother' are drawn to each other like magnets, for both are focusing on 'pregnancy'. The Universe does not understand 'want' and 'don't want'. It simply responds to the focus on 'pregnancy'.

The primary thought of a soul that has experienced many rejections over many lifetimes may be that physical life equals pain and rejection. In this case, too, a pregnancy that leads to an abortion could be the manifestation of the 'child' in question.

We cannot tell you if it is right or wrong, for ultimately, there is no right and wrong in the Universe, there is only experience, and all things experienced with another are always, always, a co-creation. The Universe does not victimise; it delivers only and always the subject of that to which attention is being given. If rejection is your point of attention, then that is what you will experience. If guilt is your point of attention, then you will manifest that which represents guilt for you, and so it is with all things. So do all things that you do with awareness; make conscious choices. An abortion can have lasting effects on you as an individual and on a family. For example, when other children are involved and an unplanned pregnancy comes along, the energy of that incoming soul has already been experienced by the 'siblings'. In this instance an abortion can lead to great feelings of loss for the children involved, even when on the conscious level they are not even aware of such a pregnancy.

> *"If guilt is your point of attention, then you will manifest that*
> *which represents guilt for you, and so it is with all things."*

Each person faced with this choice needs to know that whatever you decide, or have decided, it is fine and fitting for you, for all choices are individual. However, we encourage you to do all that you do consciously. If it is your conscious choice to terminate your pregnancy and you understand all that it is bringing you in terms of growth, then that is fine. If it is your choice instead to carry the pregnancy through to the eventual birth of a child, then that is also fine. We simply advise you to do all that you do consciously. If you have the child, celebrate and welcome the new life that has chosen to come to your world through you. If you choose to terminate, celebrate and thank this soul for assisting you to look at yourself and your choices in different ways. Only you the individual can really know why you have created such circumstances, and only you can truly know what is right for you. You cannot harm another soul, just as another soul cannot harm you. Thank and bless all your pregnancies, unwanted or not, for each event in your life is Divine grace in action.

> *"Each event in your life*
> *is Divine grace in action."*

We wish to give you another example of how souls serve one another in making life decisions. This example is not about abortion, but it does concern a case of what has been termed "cot death". A young soul left the body at just a few months old. This 'death' was a great shock to the parents and served them in many, many ways. Firstly, from the father's point of view, he was a deeply religious man who also had a sexual addiction that often involved his making inappropriate sexual contacts with children. His religiosity combined with his 'guilt' gave him strong beliefs concerning his need to be punished and his greatest fear was that 'God' would punish him for his 'deviant' behaviour.

From the mother's point of view, she was one who had great difficulty in feeling, feeling anything at all. She found it almost impossible to make a decision for herself, for she did not know how to ask herself what it was that she wanted, she could not 'feel' what she wanted. Owing to this, she had had unsatisfactory relationships in which all the authority in her life had been given to her male counterparts. Despite the fact that she felt that there was something 'wrong' with this sort of relationship, she could not act upon the thought, or felt powerless to do so. Additionally, she had traditionally seen herself as a victim, as someone to whom things simply happened. This was largely the result of being raised by a results-oriented mother who criticised her severely for not being good enough.

Both of these individuals were setting up the patterns of fear, guilt, martyrdom, and fear of punishment that can lead to such an event, and so it did. The soul of the child wanted nothing more than to 'awaken' the mother to the reality of her situation, although it had also gained the 'permission' of the father's soul in this process. This particular soul was a member of the mother's soul group, one who had indeed been a grandmother. This soul wanted to assist the mother to open up to her emotions. The death of the child prompted the thought in the mother that said, "Why didn't my child want to stay?" Clearly, the message that a 'choice' to stay or to go was involved got through to the mother, and this realisation led to other thoughts of 'why' the choice was made. In this sense, the purpose of the soul that chose to 'die' was fulfilled and this soul had assisted the mother in the best way it knew how.

For the father, this soul wanted to assist him to see that he was making choices that were damaging to him, and sought to challenge him to go to his deeper sense of guilt and fear and confront those feelings. The 'baby' had determined that this loss of a child would make clear to him the 'loss' he was creating elsewhere. This was not a punishment, for punishment does not exist. It was done out of love, in service to both the individuals involved. We understand that some of you will see the mother as the 'good guy' and the father as the 'bad guy', but in reality, there is no such differentiation. All are acceptable in the eyes of God, and all of you are creating your own experience.

By explaining to you these events in such a way, we are intending to help you see that all the painful events that occur in your life are there because you have not yet figured out a way to make life changes without getting your own attention through pain. Unfortunately, most of you don't realise that something is not working until it begins to hurt.

How does what you have said about abortion apply to euthanasia and suicide?

Let us be clear with you, your questions concerning life and death arise because you have many beliefs concerning death that do not reflect the reality of the situation. First, there is no death, you cannot die; all life, *all life*, is eternal. It cannot be any other way, and it is not any other way. Second, many of you still believe in an external 'God' that has 'given' you life. In this externalisation of

'God' you have assigned 'him' human traits, making decisions about what 'God' does and does not want, and about what is good or bad in the eyes of this 'God'. Many of you believe that 'life' was given you by 'God' and that this life should not be squandered or wasted by suicide, or that only 'God' has the right to take that life away through a 'natural' death. There are many of you who are not even contemplating suicide but who are squandering your life by not living it fully! Which is the greater crime? To make a conscious choice to leave where you are because it is no longer joyful, or to stay put and be miserable leading your life restricted by many beliefs that say you are less than who you truly are? Death comes to both; one is just quicker than the other, that is all!

The life and light of the Universe lives within you; it is not separate from you. You are the creator and the source of your own light and life, for you are the extension of God, the 'finger' of God protruding and extending into your reality. You are the highest authority in your life, no other, and it is for you to decide what is joyful and what is not. Although we would agree with you that there are other choices 'higher' than suicide, for some it is the best choice. We say this because there are some who have very successfully cornered themselves with fears and strong beliefs concerning themselves and their reality, so there is very little opportunity for them to 'break free' of the prison they have created for themselves. Certain individuals have more opportunities to solve their problems in the non-physical than the physical. We say this because in the non-physical world they will be more susceptible to the influence of other 'positive' souls, angelic beings, and guides. However, we will state clearly that physical death does not solve the 'problem', for the 'problem' has arisen out of thought, just as all creation arises out of thought. So, just as thought had created the Earth life circumstances from which the personality wished to escape, these very same thoughts will create a world that reflects those feelings in the non-physical world.

> *"You are the highest authority in your life, no other, and it is for*
> *you to decide what is joyful and what is not."*

It is not true that those who take their own lives are 'punished', but there are many cases of personalities who have committed suicide and who end up in a 'grey area' not unlike the 'purgatory' that some of your religions speak of. It is a place of 'psychological' self-imprisonment. The personality has imprisoned itself behind the walls of dark thoughts and hopelessness. However, having said this, there are those who commit suicide knowing that they will go somewhere 'better'. Because their departure is dominated by the thought of going somewhere 'better', with emotion to support it, they end up somewhere 'better' in the non-physical world. In almost all of these cases, the personality merges very successfully with the soul and the soul immediately begins planning to return to the physical plane in order to overcome the difficulties they have just abandoned. Other souls say, "I want to leave this sorrowful world." This focus on "sorrowful world" creates that very same experience in the non-physical, the 'purgatory' we have just spoken of. This experience of 'purgatory' can last in your terms for a few minutes or for several hundred years, indeed thousands. You see, you create your own reality, not some of it, not most of it, but *all of it*, both in the physical and non-physical worlds.

Although this focus can 'trap' a personality for a long time, the soul is still free to create a new experience elsewhere. The nature of the soul is that it is multidimensional. Not only does a soul exist in many different realities simultaneously, it has different aspects of itself. When a part of itself becomes self-aware, it individuates, just as a part of your soul individuated to become you. The goal of the soul is to eventually reunite with all its parts and return to the source, the Oneness of All-That-Is. However, a part of it, a personality or fragment, can be 'left' behind in 'purgatory' even while the soul has started another lifetime on Earth. In this sense, there would be a part of you here in the body on Earth and a part of you that has been separated through despair and is 'trapped' in a belief system that is not to the overall benefit of your soul. Most experienced souls will recover these 'lost' parts before embarking on a new incarnation, because these lost parts can, and often do, have an influence on the new physical incarnation. Often, this fragment may be experienced as an attachment, for the 'lost part' may try to live physical life once more through the newly incarnated personality. Many who have suspected 'possessions' or 'hauntings' are actually experiencing aspects of themselves that have yet to be reunited. This rarely happens to 'older' more experienced souls, although it can.

On the highest level, there is never right or wrong, there is only experience. Suicide is as valid a choice as any. You take with you all that you have experienced here, and it will create your experience 'there'.

With regard to euthanasia, we encourage you to act according to your own deeper sense of knowing. It is our understanding that those who request another's assistance to pass out of the physical dimension are in such deep physical distress that life appears to have no quality. If your love for that person leads you to support them and to assist them in doing what they feel is right for them, then this is what you must do. If, however, you do not feel capable of such action, then do not participate. And, as with everything, we implore you to do all that you do with awareness. Why do your beliefs challenge you? Why is it difficult for you to aid another in this way? Challenge your thoughts and your beliefs. Ask what is valid, what serves you and what does not.

We encourage you always to uplift those involved in this process. Remind them of the beauty of where they are going and of the beauty that they are leaving behind. Make their passing as comfortable as possible and support them in holding a far greater vision of who they are. You are the sovereign over your body, it is your creation, and they are the sovereign over their body and have the 'right' to dispose of it how and when they will. In essence, ALL physical death is suicide, for a soul always consents to the withdrawal of a personality when it cannot gain anything further from the experience. All physical death is caused by one thing and one thing only, and that is fear. Those who are enlightened are without fear, and they can live in their physical bodies as long as they choose. They can do so because their 'creative vortex' is fully open, and that physical organism is fed by the pure positive energy of the Universe, by the love of God. It is this energy that feeds your body, that gives you life, and it is fear that restricts the flow of this energy coming to you.

Fear is the source of all your woes, of all your diseases and of all physical death, just as fear is the cause of the aging and decay of the physical organism. Your cells replace themselves constantly. This is done to such an extent that you are literally not the same person that you were several years ago. Every cell in your body has been replaced. However, the new cells reproduce themselves and take on form according to your thinking. Therefore, if you think that you are old, or getting older, then the cells will transform themselves likewise to appear 'old' and decayed.

Resistance causes old age, disease, and death. Because you do not yet fully understand that you are the creator of your world, you still see yourself as an object to which things can simply happen. Owing to this belief, your society has set up many structures designed to 'defend' you against the incursions of all things external to you. However, because you are resisting that which is undesired, you are focusing upon it and drawing it into your experience. This gives you the 'evidence' that the Universe is indeed a dangerous place and that, in order for you to be safe and secure, you need to resist and fight against all those things that are undesirable. This resistance creates a break in the flow of pure positive energy coming towards you, for when you are saying, "No, No, No," the Universe cannot deliver that which is positive in any great quantity.

Chapter 17

Are there Other Cultures?

Are there cultures on other planets similar or more advanced than our own?

Have you seen the stars in the heaven? Can you count them? That number, and many, many more, is the number of civilisations that exist not only in your own galaxy, but in countless thousands of other galaxies. The Universe is a vast place, much more vast than you could possibly comprehend, and yet, it is all contained in oneness. It is all linked, all connected.

So many of you, when you think of cultures and civilisations on other worlds, think automatically that they must be more advanced than your own. This is not so. Each of the physical worlds is at a different stage of growth, each of them unique. To put things more succinctly in your terms, there are those worlds that are 'worse' than your own, and those worlds that are 'better' than your own. This view that, if there are civilisations out there amongst the stars, they must in some way be superior to yours, stems from your collective lack of self-appreciation. You have all convinced yourselves that you are such lowly and unworthy beings. What we want to communicate to you more than anything is the knowledge that you are acceptable, and that you do love well enough, and that you are indeed valued and cherished members of the family of God.

> "You are indeed valued and cherished members
> of the family of God."

Each world undergoes evolution. As a soul first enters the physical world, it is preoccupied with survival. When an entire world is occupied with such new souls, then this world would seem brutal and bloodthirsty as the inhabitants there see dangers and enemies around every corner. Such a world is filled with cultures that are driven by fear. As souls develop, and cultures with them, they become more organised. Religion takes on a more structured and important role, political divisions and subdivisions appear and one group exercises dominance over another; or the civilisations claim dominion over the actual physical world in which they live, very much as your culture has done. As you gain more and more experience, both individually and collectively, the Soul has greater influence over the actions of individual beings. As this happens, these cultures are transformed by a sense of unity, community and harmony. You, the Earth people, you are at this stage of development. You are currently exploring which way to go with your technology. Hitherto, you have used much of your technological prowess to enhance your military strength. However, in recent decades technology has been taking on a different role, and this role is being influenced by the soul of humanity. Your technology is being used to bring humanity together. No longer do great oceans divide you, but you are becoming a global village. As a species, you are at a major crossroads, and yes indeed, you are making the right choices, and indeed, you will 'make it'. Although it may appear as if technology is causing many problems, you will find the answers, for there are sufficient numbers of you who want to find solutions.

Some of your bothers and sisters have come to observe you at this time. Not to participate, not to influence you, or even to save you, for you need no saving. They have come to witness the marvel of humanity. To use an analogy, we are seated in a beautiful meadow gazing upon a beautiful chrysalis. The creature that went into it is rather different from the one that will emerge. We are watching the birth of a most precious and rare butterfly. That butterfly, my beloved friends, is humanity, soon ready to reach for the sky and drink in the sweet nectar of life on a warm summer's day. We celebrate your humanity, your history, and marvel at how you are unfolding your higher will and the plan for humanity in your lifetime.

Changes will not come overnight, but they are coming, for you are in the midst of them. Is not the world more compassionate now than a mere hundred years ago? Yes, of course it is. Far from being the dunces of the universe, you are graduating to the next level, to a New World of excitement. Expect not to be saved or rescued, for you do not need either, but expect that your light will shine and shine some more, for the everlasting flame lives within you and is awakening. The Universal Christ has arrived, and lives within you.

When you understand that you are connected to all life, then the time will be ripe for you to explore all the life you are connected to.

Chapter 18

Meditation

What is the importance of meditation?

Meditation has many forms and many definitions. We will define from our perspective what it is we believe you mean by the term. For some, meditation is simply spending quiet time with oneself, or indeed, even being involved in an activity such as painting or some other creative form. Meditation is about focus; as you quiet your mind and let go of all that which is unfocused, you are in a meditative state. So many of you have heard that in order to meditate you need to be in a state of 'no thought'. We do not share this view. You can, if you wish, choose just one thought, perhaps the thought of beauty, love, peace, or a visualisation of a condition that you would like to bring about in your life. This is meditation. We offer this because, as you focus on one thing, you still your mind sufficiently to allow your Inner Self, your Greater Self, your Soul, to come forth. If then, you choose your focus to be your Soul, then focus upon that desire, and that deeper connection will manifest within you.

As we have said many times, you are a finger of God protruding into your physical reality, you are an extension of that which is non-physical into the physical. Meditation, or focus, allows you to tap into those broader, greater, more expanded parts of yourself and you can do this simply by setting the intention to do so. Prior to entering into the physical, your non-physical self had an intention to live as a joyful being, in alignment with the Four Principles of Creation.

Through meditation and your intention to become aware of your non-physical self, you open an upward channel through which your Soul's energy, inspiration, and encouragement can flow. Your Soul has an intention towards love, health and well-being, abundance, and creation itself. As you align your energies with the energies of your Soul through meditation, you will come increasingly under the influence of your Soul, and thereby be assisted to create more harmony in your life. There is much celebration in the non-physical realm of your Soul when a person like you reaches upwards for inner guidance and for conscious connection. As you do this, your Soul responds with love, for it is delighted at the opportunity to work directly with you, for this fulfils its greater purpose of creating a soul-led life in the physical world. We speak at this time as if your Soul and you are separate entities, but that is not so. You are a multidimensional being, and the 'you' that you know, the one reading these words, is but a small part of your entire being. You may even hear your Soul's guidance as words, or you may feel a rush of inspiration, or feel peace about a certain aspect of your life or love where you were previously troubled.

It is important to have an intention when you meditate. Set the intention to merge with that which is greater and broader, with your Soul. As you set this intention, you summon forth your Soul, that eternal part of you that contains within it the lifetime experience of all of your lifetimes, both physical and non-physical, and much more than all this. As you tap into the broader consciousness of your Soul, you tap into the universal mind and the source of all life. Daily connection to the source of all life will greatly assist you to create a life that is more joyful and fulfilling.

Exercise:

Set aside 20 minutes and ensure that you will not be disturbed in any way. Unplug telephones and inform anyone with whom you be living that this is now your quiet time to be with yourself.

You may want to put on some soft melodic music, light a candle, create an atmosphere that is relaxing, nurturing and calming for you. Loosen your clothes, or change into those that are more comfortable.

Find a comfortable place to sit, and get into a position that you can hold for at least 15 minutes.

As you sit there, ready for your meditation, take three deep breaths, and on the exhale release all that you do not need to be with you, all thoughts that are not necessary. As you clear your energy in this way, then feel within you your intention to align with and merge with your soul. As you feel your intention to do this, state it. You can either say this out loud, or within your mind, but do state it: "I now intend to merge with my Greater Self, with my Soul." Once you have set this intention, let it go.

Close your eyes and focus on your breathing, allowing it to become restful but fairly full. Allow yourself to relax, letting your lower jaw open slightly. Now we would like you to breathe in through the nose and out through the mouth. If breathing in through the nose is difficult for you, then it is all right to breathe in through the mouth. Simply continue this breathing, and focus only on the breath. Bring your attention to your breastbone in the centre of your chest, and focus on it as you feel it rise and fall with the breath. Become breath. Breath is all that you are, you are breath. Continue to focus on the breath. If any thoughts trundle across your mind, then consciously re-focus on your breathing. Eventually, you will slip away into your inner realm.

Continue this meditation for at least 15–20 minutes. At some stage you may sense movement. This movement could be a sense of rotation within you, or your arms may feel as if they are lifting, or you may have an 'involuntary' movement of the neck. When you sense this, you know that you are deeply connected with your Soul and the movement is your Soul adjusting your energies so that you may accommodate more of it.

Do this mediation each day. Perhaps in the morning, or just as you return from work. Meditate when you feel energised, not when you feel tired, as then there will be a tendency to fall asleep. The goal here is the conscious merging with your Soul Self.

I have tried to meditate, but all I ever do is either I fall asleep or my mind starts to wander, thinking of all sorts of things that need to be done.

The mind is like any other part of your body that you intend to use for a specific purpose. It takes practice to train your mind to focus. You see, if you have never run a marathon, you would not expect your body to be able to complete the race without building up to it, would you? And so it is with meditation. As you go about your day, you are a human doing, instead of a human being. You have become accustomed to processing multiple levels of information. You drive cars, you watch the road, you listen to the radio, you speak on the cell phone, and you try to do it all at once, so your mind has little practice at simply focusing on one thing only, and you have little practice at simply being.

When you fall asleep during meditation, it is simply because you are reaching those levels of consciousness that you are not accustomed to interpreting in the awakened state. As you fall asleep, you withdraw your focus from the material into the inner world. Some have called this the dreamscape. Through meditation, you begin to pierce this veil and venture into the dreamscape, into the inner world. However, your conscious mind does yet not know how to interpret this information for you, so you experience blackout. If the blackout lasts for any longer than a few seconds, or a minute or so, you generally fall off to sleep.

You simply need to train your mind to focus, for that is all that is needed in order to meditate, even if it means focusing on the void or on silence. You can train yourself to focus on an object, such as a candle or a flower. You can perhaps time yourself. First try for 3 minutes, then 5 minutes, then 7 minutes, working your way upward to 15 minutes. Each time you are able to quiet your mind chatter and simply focus on one thing, you allow the influence of your Inner Self, your Soul to come forth.

Another way to practice focus is to focus on something you want to create. Creative visualisation is an excellent way to pave the way for deeper meditation. You can simply select something that you would like to have more of in your life, sit, and focus on that thought for a minimum of 15 minutes. As you do this, observe how the thought has a natural evolution to it. Notice how the original thought changes and the vision becomes bigger and new ideas become added to the subject of your focus. This is conscious daydreaming, something we recommend that each of you do daily. Set aside time for yourself each day, at least 15–20 minutes. Sit in a comfortable chair and choose the topic of your conscious dream. Perhaps it is a dream about drawing a new love into your life, or of adding more health and vitality, financial abundance, a new home or job. Once you have chosen your subject, begin to visualise the best-case scenario. As you do this, allow your feelings of excitement to well up within you and see how the dream changes. This kind of visualising is not only good for training the mind to focus on one subject and one subject only, it is a powerful way to launch new creations in your life.

If your mind wanders, simply refocus back on your dream. If the wandering persists, write down the things that have come up in your dream, so that you can rest knowing that you can return to them.

Meditation is much easier than most of you suppose. Not only is it much easier, it is a powerful and fruitful way to forge links with your Inner Self. As you forge stronger links to your inner world, your outer world will begin to change. You will be in closer contact with your dreams, with your desires, and you will have a sense of purpose. Meditation will accelerate your spiritual growth and will create a space for many new things to come to you.

Some are tempted to use meditation as a way to withdraw from the physical world. Although there is great value in doing that momentarily, the purpose of meditation is for you to strengthen the connection to your Soul, so that your Soul may be fully present on the Earth plane. We would suggest that 20 minutes once or twice a day is sufficient. There are many aids available to you, guided meditations, meditation music, and courses of all kinds. Choose your time and the method that suits you. Simply remember the spirit of what you are doing, which is to form a stronger connection to your inner world, to the greater part of who you are.

A Final Word

As a final word to all that has been said thus far in this volume, we encourage you, as always, to follow your deep inner feelings. We have observed that so many of you are concerned that you may be getting things wrong, concerned about what truth is, what to believe, what not to believe. We say to you again, let your heart decide. If something feels good, if it elevates your vision of yourself and of humanity, then that is truth. Again we encourage you to take only those things in this volume that speak to you directly into your heart, and leave the rest for further consideration.

Perhaps when deciding whether what you read or hear is true, you could ask yourself, "What would love do?" When you understand that love is acceptance and freedom, then you can understand how love communicates.

We seek to remind you once more that you are truly loved. That you were created in love and that love is what governs your entire existence. There is nothing wrong with you, or with humanity or with this planet. Each of you is in the physical world through free choice, not to prove yourself worthy of some higher being or hierarchy, but to create and to experience the fullness of your being whilst in the physical dimension. You are the creator and attractor of your experience and thus you came forth into the physical to create and to attract in this reality just as you have already done in many other realities and dimensions.

Your deepest desire is to create your life in accordance with the Four Principles of Creation – Love, Health & Well Being, Abundance and Creativity. Trust your inner feelings; trust what feels good, for what feels good is the measurement of your success. There are no rights or wrongs, but only meanderings along the path of experience towards that which fulfills, inspires and energizes you. Enjoy life! Celebrate life! All is well with you and with your world, really, it is!

We come forth with a perspective and with answers, as long as there are those who have questions. Therefore, if after having read this volume you have been stimulated to much thought and have more questions, please ask!

Blessed be, beloved ones. Enjoy the journey!

Omni-Emmanuel

If you would like to contribute to further works by Omni, please send your questions to info@four-principles.com. (Personal questions cannot be considered.)

For information on seminars, lectures, tapes and therapies offered by John Payne and Omni, contact info@four-principles.com.

Acknowledgements

To René Penders – thank you for all that was good between us, this I take into my heart. My deepest gratitude goes to the consciousness, the soul, that comes to me in the form of my dog Bo-Bo, I want you to know that you have given me more joy than you could imagine.

With many thanks to the entire nation of South Africa, you have given me gifts that are so precious; you will always have a special place in my heart. Special thanks to my many friends in South Africa: Lorna Rose Wheaton – for your love, Sandy Bruck – for your humour, tact and natural wisdom, Gina Furness – just simply for being you "I love you to life", Pam Summers and Bev Moss – for showing me what courage is, Mark Schorn, for your generosity. And a special thank you to Hilda de la Rosa, good friend, teacher, confident – thank you for reminding me who I really am. Also thank you to Monica Minutelli, Peter Jordaan, Peter Wheaton, Donald Craig and Susan Hojdar

Across the ocean now to the USA. A very, very special thanks you to Sue Layel, a precious friend, thank you for your encouragement and for believing in my work. Also thank you to all of you who have supported me with your generosity and encouragement: Pam Krueger, Susan Sarao, Colleen Clarke, Helga Torda, Catherine O'Connor, Laura Turlington, Dr Nan Seedman and many more. A very special thank you to Judee Pouncey. My deepest gratitude goes to Barney Stein in New York, his capacity for generosity, love and support have moved me deeply!

On home territory now in Europe… in Germany I would like to thank Dr Horst Schöll and Helga Schöll for providing the platform for me to start teaching. Also, many, many thanks to Corinne Würfel and Uwe Stein.

In Norway, my thanks go to Trine Simmenes and her mother Jane, thanks for providing not only support of my work, but the most idyllic place to stay. That Fjord just has to be seen!

In Croatia, thank you to Vedran Kraljeta for his efforts and his wife Vesna for her hospitality and good cooking! Also thank you to Mara and Lydia.

Finally, in The Netherlands, a big, big thank you to Ans Kuijpers. Thank you for being there! Your heart is truly golden. Also a thank you to Renée Bost for your love and support.

I would like to acknowledge my dear, dear friend Biene Haagsma (nee Annebiene Pilon). You are a true healer, many thanks for your love and support. Also, to my dear friend Paulo Monica – thank you. Words cannot express how blessed I feel to have you both in my life, I love you.

Also thank you to Thierry Bogliolo, my publisher at Findhorn, for his encouragement and rapid acceptance of my work.

I would also like to thank my spiritual teachers who have touched my life with their outstanding work, Sanaya Roman, Duane Packer and Lindsay Senecal. Also, Pantha Haring and Marijke Schneider-Blomjous. I also pay tribute to Jane Roberts, Louise Hay, Deepak Chopra, Oprah Winfrey, Marianne Williamson and others who have been pioneers of our time and servants to humanity. These souls have my deepest respect and gratitude.

Finally, I bless and thank my parents Donald Victor Payne and Lourdes Clemencia Bebeagua for providing me with the perfect environment in which I could acquire all the skills that I have today. Thank you for making my life so very, very rich. Thank you for all the countries you took me to live in! And thank you for your love, I receive it gladly.

Index

Notes

.

Notes

Notes

Notes

Notes

Notes

FINDHORN Press

Findhorn Press is the publishing business of the Findhorn Community which has grown around the Findhorn Foundation in northern Scotland.

For further information about the Findhorn Foundation and the Findhorn Community, please contact:

Findhorn Foundation
The Visitors Centre
The Park, Findhorn IV36 3TY, Scotland, UK
tel 01309 690311• fax 01309 691301
email reception@findhorn.org
www.findhorn.org

For a complete Findhorn Press catalogue, please contact:

Findhorn Press

The Park, Findhorn,	P. O. Box 13939
Forres IV36 3TY	Tallahassee
Scotland, UK	Florida 32317-3939, USA
Tel 01309 690582	~~Tel (850) 893-2920~~
freephone 0800-389-9395	to~~ll-free 1-877-390-4425~~
Fax 01309 690036	~~Fax (850) 893-3442~~

e-mail info@findhornpress.com
http://www.findhornpress.com

Books by Marko Pogačnik

Marko Pogačnik, born in 1944 in Kranj, Slovenia, studied sculpture and acquired an international reputation in conceptual and landscape art. He has developed this further into 'earth lithopuncture', which aims at healing disturbed landscapes and power points. He leads seminars in earth healing in several countries and provides advice on landscape matters for communities and businesses. Marko Pogačnik is a lecturer at the Hagia Chora School for Geomancy, which was founded in 1995.

Nature Spirits & Elemental Beings:
Working with the Intelligence in Nature
ISBN 1-899171-66-5

This book is remarkable in that almost everything described in the book is based on the author's own practical experiences in communicating with these beings through meditation and tuning into plants, trees, animals and the landscape. He describes in detail the various elemental beings and their roles in maintaining the web of life, and also gives insights into related topics, such as the flow of energies within landscape, and the long-suppressed Goddess culture. His evocative images of the nature spirits draw our attention to the lost harmony of the natural world which has been disrupted by the impact of human culture.

"It is not that is is difficult to put down, for much of its material cries out to be pondered and compared with experience; rather one returns to it in the joyful anticipation of new insights, and hope is not disappointed."
—Gnosis

"There are many fascinating insights to be found on the nature of life and the modern relevance of folktales and legends. The style is so personable and unaffected that most doubts as to authencity are pushed aside. A most fascinating and worthwhile read."
—Kindred Spirit

"This is a remarkable book by one of Europe's most important spiritual teachers. It provides unique and entertaining insights into the world of earth spirits and fairy folk. This is important information for the imagination and for healing the earth."
—William Bloom

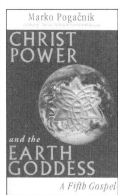

Christ Power and the Earth Goddess:
A Fifth Gospel
ISBN 1-899171-92-4

Marko Pogačnik has always been convinced that there existed a fifth Gospel, one that would be relevant for the challenges facing humanity as it enters the third millennium.

Here we have stories filled with the excitement of a detective book, where the author researches and investigates and travels to distant lands. Using his remarkable investigative powers, Pogacnik discovered this new Gospel composed of separate messages woven into the text of the canonical Gospels. These offer perspectives sharply different from the usual biblical interpretations. They speak of love and wholeness, male and female, and the union and communion of all humanity with the Earth and the realms of Angels. The dualism of good and evil has no part in them. Pogačnik concludes that the Fifth Gospel was edited out of the canonical texts, either because their message was too far removed from contemporary understanding, or because they interfered with plans for the formal, hierarchical theo-political structure which we know as the Church. Yet these lost messages of Jesus are deeply meaningful for our present time and our transition to the next stage of our evolution.

The choice is ours. We can move forward as one to a new plane of evolution, reconnect with the Christ Power that is in each one of us, and create a communion with our Planet Earth. Love, reconciliation and the consciousness of the heart will be our guiding stars in the coming days. In the words of Jesus himself, we can create Heaven on Earth.

Earth Changes, Human Destiny:
Coping and Attuning with the Help of the Revelation of St John
ISBN 1-899171-53-3

Marko Pogačnik's previous books have brought the reader into an ever closer relationship with the true Spirit of Nature. This latest work tells of currently on-going changes in Earth's constitution and presents simple exercises by which the reader can adjust her or his vibrations to the changing ones of Earth and Heaven. Our human participation is essential to help Earth through the birth trauma — giving birth to her true self — and to ensure our continued evolution as part of the planetary process.

Marko Pogačnik enlightens his conclusions with a study of the Biblical Revelation of St. John — also known as The Apocalypse. This turns out to be, not a prophecy of the End of Time beloved of doomsayers, but the story of a New Beginning. As always, Pogačnik presents his observations with the precision of a scientist, so that they are measurable and replicable. The changes in Earth's constitution are beginning to appear on the physical level and this book is necessary reading for all who would keep pace with their effects on their own personal body and emotions. In doing so they will help the larger whole.

"In this millennial moment Marko Pogačnik brings us transformative understanding and practices to heal the deep, life-threatening split in our western psyche: the split between body and soul, between sacred nature and spiritual gnosis. His work and guidance are priceless for us now."
—Sidney Lanier, co-founder with Barbara Marx-Hubbard, Foundation for Conscious Evolution.

Healing the Heart of the Earth:
Restoring the Subtle Levels of Life
ISBN 1-899171-57-6

Thanks to the global ecological movement, people everywhere have begun to realize the destructive consequences of our civilization's uncontrolled development. This book takes the next step and directs public awareness to the destructive processes that, almost unnoticed, endanger the invisible subtle systems of nature, the landscape and life on earth. What actually happens to the earth when one of its heart chakras is ruthlessly blocked by a building that has been erected without sensitivity? When a wall with a 'no-man's-land' cuts an integral landscape into two (the Berlin Wall, which still stands despite having been physically dismantled)? When massive constructions of steel and concrete slice through the sensitive energy lines of the earth (road networks)? All this leads to blockages and imbalances in the subtle organs and energy systems of the earth which culminate in a life-endangering malfunction.